D0436499

The Uncommon Wisdom of JFK

A PORTRAIT IN HIS OWN WORDS

Edited by BILL ADLER

Editor of The Kennedy Wit

Also edited by

BILL ADLER

The Kennedy Wit

*The Uncommon Wisdom of
Jacqueline Kennedy Onassis*

RUGGED LAND | 276 CANAL STREET · FIFTH FLOOR · NEW YORK CITY · NY 10013 · USA

RuggedLand

PUBLISHED BY RUGGED LAND, LLC

276 CANAL STREET · NEW YORK · NY · 10013 · USA

RUGGED LAND AND COLOPHON ARE TRADEMARKS OF RUGGED LAND, LLC.

LIBRARY OF CONGRESS CONTROL NUMBER 2003108906

PUBLISHER'S CATALOGING-IN-PUBLICATION DATA

Kennedy, John F. (John Fitzgerald), 1917-1963.
The uncommon wisdom of John F. Kennedy : a portrait in his own words /
John F. Kennedy ; edited by Bill Adler ; produced by Tom Folsom. – 1st ed.
p. cm.
LCCN 2003108906
ISBN 1-59071-015-0
1. Kennedy, John F. (John Fitzgerald), 1917-1963--Quotations.
2. Presidents--United States--Quotations.
I. Adler, Bill, 1929- II. Folsom, Tom. III. Title.

E 838.5.K42 2003   973.922'092
QBI03-200542

Book Design by
HSU + ASSOCIATES

RUGGED LAND WEBSITE ADDRESS: WWW.RUGGEDLAND.COM

OCTOBER 2003

1 3 5 7 9 10 8 6 4 2
FIRST EDITION

Contents

The Uncommon Wisdom of John F. Kennedy

Introduction

I never met President John F. Kennedy. I wish I had. But his words, whether in his speeches, in his writing, or off the cuff, always resonated with me—they resonated back in 1964 when I wrote *The New York Times* bestseller *The Kennedy Wit,* and they resonate even more so today.

To commemorate the fortieth anniversary of that tragic day in Dallas, I have put together this book of the wisdom and wit of John F. Kennedy. It tells the story of his life and his presidency—in his own words.

Many books have been written about President Kennedy, but no author could possibly capture the spirit of this man's life and work better than he did himself.

BILL ADLER

New York City 2003

An Uncommon Man

"**If** we are strong, our strength will speak for itself. If we are weak, words will be of no help."

"Only those who dare to fail greatly can ever achieve greatly."

"If a free society cannot help the many who are poor, it cannot save the few who are rich."

"What we do in this country, the kind of society that we build, that will tell whether freedom will be sustained around the world."

"Do not pray for easy lives. Pray to be stronger men."

The Uncommon Wisdom of John F. Kennedy

"In the long history of the world, only a few generations have been granted the role of defending freedom in its hour of maximum danger. I do not shrink from this responsibility—I welcome it."

"Those who make peaceful revolution impossible will make violent revolution inevitable."

"We in this country, in this generation, are—by destiny rather than choice—the watchmen on the walls of world freedom."

"Give me your help and your hand, and your voice and your vote."

"Freedom is indivisible, and when one man is enslaved, all are not free."

"All free men, wherever they may live, are citizens of Berlin. And therefore, as a free man, I take pride in the words *'Ich bin ein Berliner.'*"

"And so, my fellow Americans: ask not what

your country can do for you—ask what you can
do for your country."

The Uncommon Wisdom of John F. Kennedy

The Run for
the Presidency

John Fitzgerald Kennedy was born on May 29, 1917, at 83 Beals Street in Brookline, Massachusetts, to Joseph and Rose Kennedy. John was named for Rose's father, John Francis Fitzgerald, the popular mayor of Boston.

After graduating from Harvard, Kennedy had planned to become a writer or a teacher. But following the death of his older brother, Joe Jr., in World War II, the family's political aspirations fell to John. Joseph Kennedy convinced his son to run for a seat in the Eleventh Congressional District of Massachusetts. Thus began the political career of John F. Kennedy.

Kennedy served three terms in the House of Representatives, and in 1952 was elected to the U.S. Senate.

8   Even in his college days, there was a sense that big things were in store for the young man. In his college senior thesis, *Why England Slept*, to prepare America for its own possible future crises, Kennedy analyzed why England found itself almost completely unprepared for World War II–"in studying the reasons why England slept, let us try to profit by them and save ourselves her anguish," he wrote. The thesis was turned into a bestselling book, and it served as a foundation for Kennedy's understanding of and reputation on foreign policy.

In the book, Kennedy explained his view that democracy is a system of government expressly designed for peace:

"In the first place, democracy is essentially peace-loving; the people don't want to go to war. When they do go, it is with a very firm conviction, because they must believe deeply and strongly in their cause before they consent.

This gives them an advantage over a totalitarian system, where the people may find themselves in a war in which they only half believe.

"For the long run, then, democracy is superior. But for the short run, democracy has great weaknesses. When it competes with a system of government which cares nothing for permanency, a system built primarily for war, democracy, which is built primarily for peace, is at a disadvantage. And democracy must recognize its weaknesses; it must learn to safeguard its institutions if it hopes to survive."

K ennedy won a Pulitzer Prize for his book *Profiles in Courage,* which he wrote in 1955 while recovering from back surgery. The book discusses the careers of eight senators who had shown remarkable courage by taking unpopular stands in support of the principles in which they believed. Kennedy wrote eloquently about valor, bravery, and the triumph of belief over public pressures:

"For without belittling the courage with which men have died, we should not forget those acts of courage with which men...have lived.... A man does what he must–in spite of personal consequences, in spite of obstacles and dangers and pressures–and that is the basis of all human morality."

"We have not fully recognized the difficulty facing a politician conscientiously desiring, in [Daniel] Webster's words, 'to push [his] skiff from the shore alone' into a hostile and turbulent sea."

"It is the politicians who see things in similar shades that have a depressing and worrisome time of it."

"Each man remains something of an enigma... shadowed by a veil which cannot be torn away."

After an unsuccessful bid for the Democratic Party's vice presidential nomination in 1956, Senator Kennedy decided he was no longer interested in the country's second-highest post. When a friend insisted that Kennedy wouldn't have the slightest problem in gaining the vice presidential nomination in 1960, he smiled and said, "Let's not talk so much about vice. I'm against vice in any form."

Instead, he decided to seek the 1960 presidential nomination.

"Several nights ago, I dreamed that the good Lord touched me on the shoulder and said, 'Don't worry, you'll be the Democratic presidential nominee in 1960. What's more, you'll be elected.' I told [U.S. Senator] Stu Symington about my dream. 'Funny thing,' said Stu, 'I had the same dream myself.' We both told our dreams to Lyndon Johnson, and Johnson said, 'That's funny. For the life of me, I can't remember tapping either of you two boys for the job.'"

Senator John F. Kennedy announced his candidacy for the presidency on January 2, 1960, in the Senate Caucus Room in Washington, D.C.

"For eighteen years, I have been in the service of the United States, first as a naval officer in the Pacific during World War II and for the past fourteen years as a member of the Congress. In the last twenty years, I have traveled in nearly every continent and country–from Leningrad to Saigon, from Bucharest to Lima. From all of this, I have developed an image of America as fulfilling a noble and historic role as the defender of freedom in a time of maximum peril–and of the American people as confident, courageous, and persevering. It is with this image that I begin this campaign."

Two weeks later, at the National Press Club in Washington, D.C., Kennedy delivered a speech on the nature of the American presidency and the role of the president over the next four years. His sense of what the sixties would later become for the nation was prescient.

"In the decade that lies ahead—in the challenging revolutionary sixties—the American presidency will demand more than ringing manifestoes issued from the rear of the battle. It will demand that the president place himself in the very thick of the fight, that he care passionately about the fate of the people he leads, that he be willing to serve them, at the risk of incurring their momentary displeasure."

"Whatever the political affiliation of our next president, whatever his views may be on all the issues and problems that rush in upon us, he must above all be the chief executive in every sense of the word. He must be prepared to exercise the fullest powers of his office—all that are specified and some that are not.... He must reopen channels of communication between the world of thought and the seat of power."

"How much better it would be, in the turbulent sixties, to have a Roosevelt or a Wilson than to have another James Buchanan, cringing in the White House, afraid to move."

16   On July 15, 1960, at the Memorial Coliseum in Los Angeles, John F. Kennedy formally accepted the Democratic Party nomination for the presidency of the United States with a speech outlining his plans for a "New Frontier."

"For the problems are not all solved and the battles are not all won—and we stand today on the edge of a New Frontier—the frontier of the 1960s—a frontier of unknown opportunities and perils—a frontier of unfulfilled hopes and threats....The New Frontier of which I speak is not a set of promises—it is a set of challenges. It sums up not what I intend to offer the American people, but what I intend to ask of them. It appeals to their pride, not to their pocketbook—it holds out the promise of more sacrifice instead of more security."

"But I tell you the New Frontier is here, whether we seek it or not. Beyond that frontier are the uncharted areas of science and space, unsolved problems of peace and war, unconquered pockets of ignorance and prejudice, unanswered questions of poverty and surplus. It would be easier to shrink back from that frontier, to look to the safe mediocrity of the past, to be lulled by good intentions and high rhetoric–and those who prefer that course should not cast their votes for me, regardless of party."

"My call is to the young in heart, regardless of age–to all who respond to the scriptural call: 'Be strong and of a good courage; be not afraid, neither be thou dismayed.'* For courage–not complacency–is our need today–leadership–not salesmanship....We can have faith in the future only if we have faith in ourselves."

"Can a nation organized and governed such as ours endure? That is the real question. Have we the nerve and the will? Can we carry through in an age where we will witness not only new

---

*Joshua 1:9

The Uncommon Wisdom of John F. Kennedy

breakthroughs in weapons of destruction–but also a race for mastery of the sky and the rain, the ocean and the tides, the far side of space and the inside of men's minds?"

"As we face the coming challenge, we, too, shall wait upon the Lord, and ask that he renew our strength. Then shall we be equal to the test. Then we shall not be weary. And then we shall prevail."

K ennedy's Republican challenger in the race was the outgoing vice president, Richard M. Nixon.

As he formally accepted the Democratic Party nomination for the presidency of the United States in 1960, Kennedy said of Nixon:

"We know that it will not be easy to campaign against a man who has spoken or voted on every known side of every known issue. Mr. Nixon may feel it is his turn now, after the New Deal and the Fair Deal–but before he deals, someone had better cut the cards."

"We are not here to curse the darkness, but to light the candle that can guide us through that darkness to a safe and sane future. For the world is changing. The old era is ending. The old ways will not do."

"The Republican nominee-to-be, of course, is also a young man. But his approach is as old as McKinley. His party is the party of the past. His speeches are generalities from *Poor Richard's Almanac*. Their platform, made up of leftover Democratic planks, has the courage of our old convictions. Their pledge is a pledge to the status quo—and today there can be no status quo."

In August 1960, referring to the famous "kitchen debate" in which Nixon had managed to argue with Soviet leader Nikita Khrushchev in a Moscow kitchen, Kennedy quipped, "Mr. Nixon may be very experienced in kitchen debates. So are a great many other married men I know."

"Mr. Nixon in the last seven days has called me an economic ignoramus, a Pied Piper, and all the rest. I've just confined myself to calling him a Republican, but he says that is getting low."

"Do you realize the responsibility I carry? I'm the only person standing between Nixon and the White House."

"We had an interesting convention at Los Angeles and we ended with a strong Democratic platform which we called 'The Rights of Man.' The Republican platform has also been presented. I do not know its title, but it has been referred to as 'The Power of Positive Thinking.'"

"A reporter asked President Eisenhower about a month ago what suggestions and ideas [Vice President] Nixon has had, and the president said, 'Give me a week and I will let you know.'"

Speaking at the Beverly Hilton Hotel in Los Angeles, just five days before the 1960 election, Kennedy defended his criticisms of Vice President Nixon and the Eisenhower administration:

"Abraham Lincoln once said, 'He has the right to criticize who has the heart to help.' We criticize, but we are going to help."

22 Television entered the world of politics during the 1960 presidential campaign. More than 66 million Americans watched the first of four televised Kennedy-Nixon presidential debates on September 26, 1960. Viewers were able to see and hear a confident, charismatic Kennedy debate against Nixon, who had just been released from the hospital following a knee injury. Later, commenting on his young, tan competitor who had been campaigning in California just before the debate, Nixon wrote, "I had never seen him looking so fit."

From the beginning of the first debate, Kennedy spoke with a mixture of urgency and optimism:

"The kind of country we have here, the kind of society we have, the kind of strength we build in the United States, will be the defense of freedom. If we do well here, if we meet our obligations, if we're moving ahead, then I think freedom will be secure around the world. If we fail, then freedom fails."

"I don't want historians, ten years from now, to say, these were the years when the tide ran out for the United States. I want them to say these were the years when the tide came in; these were the years when the United States started to move again."

The second Kennedy-Nixon presidential debate aired on October 7, 1960. Kennedy assured a listening audience of more than 61 million Americans that equal education would be a priority in his administration:

"These are the great questions: equality of education in school. About two percent of our population of white people are...illiterate, ten percent of our colored population. Sixty to seventy percent of our colored children do not finish high school. These are the questions in these areas that the North and South, East and

West are entitled to know. What will be the leadership of the president in these areas to provide equality of opportunity for employment? Equality of opportunity in the field of housing, which could be done on all federal supported housing by a stroke of the president's pen. What will be done to provide equality of education in all sections of the United States? Those are the questions to which the president must establish a moral tone and moral leadership. And I can assure you that if I'm elected president we will do so."

With his trademark blend of honesty and optimism, Kennedy remarked:

"If they elect me president, I will do my best to carry the United States through a difficult period; but I would not want people to elect me because I promised them the easy, soft life. I think it's going to be difficult; but I'm confident that this country can meet its responsibilities."

"I want people all over the world to look to the United States again, to feel that we're on the move, to feel that our high noon is in the future."

A fourth and final debate aired on October 21, 1960. The topic was foreign affairs.

"Which system, communism or freedom, will triumph in the next five or ten years? That's what should concern us, not the history of ten, or fifteen, or twenty years ago. But are we doing enough in these areas? What are freedom's chances in those areas? By 1965 or 1970, will there be other Cubas in Latin America? Will Guinea and Ghana, which have now voted with the Communists frequently as newly independent countries of Africa—will there be others? Will the Congo go Communist? Will other countries? Are we doing enough in that area? And what about Asia? Is India going to win the economic struggle or is China going to win it? Who will dominate Asia in the next five or ten years? Communism? The Chinese? Or will freedom? The question which we have to decide as Americans—are we doing enough today? Is our strength and prestige rising? Do people want to be identified with us? Do they want to follow United States leadership? I don't think they do, enough. And that's what concerns me."

"What we do in this country, the kind of society that we build, that will tell whether freedom will be sustained around the world."

"I think we have to revitalize our society. I think we have to demonstrate to the people of the world that we're determined in this free country of ours to be first–not first if, and not first but, and not first when–but first. And when we are strong and when we are first, then freedom gains; then the prospects for peace increase; then the prospects for our society gain."

"Franklin Roosevelt said in 1936 that that generation of Americans had a rendezvous with destiny. I believe in 1960 and sixty-one and two and three we have a rendezvous with destiny. And I believe it incumbent upon us to be the defenders of the United States and the defenders of freedom; and to do that, we must give this country leadership and we must get America moving again."

K ennedy on his campaign mission:

"Our task is not merely one of itemizing Republican failures. Nor is that wholly necessary. For the families forced from the farm will know how to vote without our telling them. The unemployed miners and textile workers will know how to vote. The old people without medical care–the families without a decent home–the parents of children without adequate food or schools–they all know that it's time for a change."

"The great trouble with American politics today is that we talk in slogans too often and symbols and we fight old battles. The sixties are going to be entirely different....We are a new generation...which will require new solutions."

"Not since the days of Woodrow Wilson has any candidate spoken on the presidency itself before the votes have been irrevocably cast. Let us hope that the 1960 campaign, in addition to discussing the familiar issues where our positions too often blur, will also talk about the presidency itself, as an instrument for dealing with those issues, as an office with varying roles, powers, and limitations."

"In a campaign very much like this, one hundred years ago, when the issues were the same, [Abraham Lincoln] wrote to a friend, 'I know there is a God, and I know He hates injustice. I see the storm coming and I know His hand is in it. But if He has a place and a part for me, I believe that I am ready.' Now, one hundred years later, when the issue is still freedom or slavery, we know there is a God and we know He hates injustice. We see the storm coming, and we know His hand is in it. But if He has a place and a part for me, I believe that we are ready."

From a television address on July 4, 1960: "It is time for a new generation of leadership, to cope with new problems and new opportunities. For there is a new world to be won."

At a Gridiron Dinner in Washington, Kennedy joked, "I have just received the following telegram from my generous Daddy. It says, 'Dear Jack: Don't buy a single vote more than is necessary. I'll be damned if I'm going to pay for a landslide.'"

A fellow Democrat introduced Kennedy at a campaign rally in Muskegon, Michigan, with tremendous enthusiasm. Kennedy began his speech:

"I want to express my appreciation to the governor. Every time he introduces me as the potentially greatest president in the history of the United States, I always think perhaps he is overstating it one or two degrees. George Washington wasn't a bad president and I do want to say a word for Thomas Jefferson. But, otherwise, I will accept the compliment."

Throughout the campaign, some wondered whether the young senator had the necessary experience to lead the nation. He reminded the skeptics:

"For fourteen years I have placed my confidence in the citizens of Massachusetts—and they have generously responded by placing their confidence in me."

In Grand View, Missouri:

"I shook hands coming over here tonight with some farmers—and how can you tell that they are farmers? It is because their hands are twice as big. I don't know what they do with them all day, but they are twice as big because they work longer and harder than anybody, with the possible exception of candidates for the presidency."

At a whistle stop in Des Moines, Iowa, Kennedy was asked what qualifications he would look for in the person he would select for the next Secretary of Agriculture. His reply:

"First, I think he should have been at some part of his life a farmer. Secondly, I think he should live in the Midwest United States. Thirdly, he should believe that his responsibility is to preserve the family farm and not liquidate it. Fourth, and finally, it would be helpful if he were a Democrat."

In Palmer, Alaska, Kennedy pointed out:

"I am the first candidate for the presidency to actively campaign in the state of Alaska. There are three electoral votes in Alaska. I left Washington, D.C., this morning at eight o'clock. I have come, I figure, about three thousand miles per electoral vote. And if I travel eight hundred thousand miles in the next two months, we might win this election."

In New York City:

"I remember reading when I was in school that at a rally in Madison Square Garden when President Roosevelt was running for a second term they unfolded a great sign that said, 'We love him for the enemies he has made.' Well, I have been making some good enemies lately. I find it a rather agreeable experience."

At a press conference in Seattle, Washington:

QUESTION: Senator, do you feel that strong personalities, such as President Eisenhower and Governor Rockefeller, campaigning against you will be perhaps a severe handicap in your campaign?

KENNEDY: No.

QUESTION: Why?

KENNEDY: I think that President Eisenhower is not running this year, and Governor Rockefeller was not nominated. I agree that President Eisenhower would be a strong candidate if he was running.

After a reporter asked Kennedy sarcastically, "Do you think a Protestant can be elected president in 1960?" he answered quickly: "If he's prepared to answer [where] he stands on the issue of the separation of church and state, I see no reason why we should discriminate against him."

"There is no city in the United States in which I get a warmer welcome and fewer votes than Columbus, Ohio."

In Phoenix, Arizona:

"I understand that [Arizona] Senator Goldwater sent a wire to Nelson Rockefeller a few days ago saying Arizona is in the bag. Well, it seems to me it is a mighty thin bag."

In Springfield, Illinois:

"What are we going to do with the Republicans? They can point to Benjamin Harrison, who according to legend saw a man forced by the Depression to eat grass on the White House lawn and had only one suggestion for him—that he go around to the back, where the grass was longer."

In New York City, a few days before the election, he referred to Governor Thomas Dewey, a Republican who unexpectedly lost the presidential election of 1948 to Harry S. Truman:

"I understand that Tom Dewey has just joined Dick Nixon out on the Coast, to give him some last-minute strategy on how to win an election."

"Ladies and gentlemen, I was warned to be out of here in plenty of time to permit those who are going to the Green Bay Packers game to leave. I don't mind running against Mr. Nixon, but I have the good sense not to run against the Green Bay Packers."

In Rockford, Illinois:

"This isn't the way they told me it was when I first decided to run for the presidency. After reading about the schedules of the president, I thought we all stayed in bed until ten or eleven and then got out and drove around."

Thanking a Los Angeles crowd for an enthusiastic reception: "I appreciate your welcome. As the cow said to the Maine farmer, 'Thank you for a warm hand on a cold morning.' "

Many claimed that Kennedy lacked the experience that many deemed necessary for the president. On the campaign trail in Minneapolis, he cleverly deflected the accusation: "Ladies and gentlemen, the outstanding news story of this week was not the events of the United Nations or even the presidential campaign. It was a story coming out of my own city of Boston that Ted Williams of the Boston Red Sox had retired from baseball. It seems that at forty-two, he was too old. It shows that perhaps experience isn't enough."

Kennedy often referred to the achievements of his young predecessors:

"To exclude from positions of trust and command all those below the age of forty-four would have kept Jefferson from writing the Declaration of Independence, Washington from commanding the Continental Army, Madison from fathering the Constitution, Hamilton from serving as Secretary of the Treasury, Clay from being elected Speaker of the House and Christopher Columbus from discovering America."

Wherever he spoke, Kennedy attracted substantial numbers of young people. Speaking in Girard, Ohio, he joked about a particularly young audience: "If we can lower the voting age to nine, we are going to sweep the state."

At the University of Michigan:

"I do not apologize for asking for your support in this campaign. I come here tonight asking your support for this country over the next decade."

To a group of young voters in a speech at East Los Angeles College: "Give me your help and your hand, and your voice and your vote."

Senator Kennedy's campaign speeches were often sprinkled with quotes from famous poets. He sometimes closed a campaign speech with a few lines from a poem by Robert Frost. While speaking before students at New York University one evening, Kennedy concluded with lines from Frost's "Stopping by Woods on a Snowy Evening"–"But I have promises to keep/And miles to go before I sleep/And miles to go before I sleep." He then paused and said, "And now I go to Brooklyn."*

---

*Another of Kennedy's favorite poems was Frost's "The Road Not Taken." The famous last lines from that poem: "Two roads diverged in a wood, and I–I took the one less traveled by, and that has made all the difference."

The Inauguration

John F. Kennedy was elected the thirty-fifth president of the United States on November 8, 1960, narrowly defeating Nixon in the closest presidential race since 1888. In winning 49.72 percent of the popular vote and 56.4 percent of the electoral vote, Kennedy became, at the age of forty-three, the youngest man ever elected president, as well as the nation's first Roman Catholic in the Oval Office.

After a heavy snowfall on the eve of Inauguration Day, President Kennedy attended morning mass at Holy Trinity Catholic Church in the Georgetown neighborhood of Washington, D.C. He then traveled to the Capitol with President Eisenhower, where Chief Justice Earl Warren administered the oath of office. President Kennedy delivered his inaugural address, which included the defining question posed to the American people: "And so, my fellow Americans: ask not what your country can do for you—ask what you can do for your country."*

40   Kennedy was optimistic about America's future in his inaugural address:

"We observe today not a victory of party but a celebration of freedom—symbolizing an end as well as a beginning—signifying renewal as well as change....The world is very different now. For man holds in his mortal hands the power to abolish all forms of human poverty and all forms of human life. And yet the same revolutionary beliefs for which our forebears fought are still at issue around the globe—the belief that the rights of man come not from the generosity of the state but from the hand of God."

"Let the word go forth from this time and place, to friend and foe alike, that the torch has been passed to a new generation of Americans, born in this century, tempered by war, dis-

---

*
Kennedy's inspiration may have been Oliver Wendell Holmes Sr., whose Memorial Day Address in 1884 included: "It is now the moment ... to recall what our country has done for each of us, and to ask ourselves what we can do for our country in return."

---

ciplined by a hard and bitter peace, proud of our ancient heritage, and unwilling to witness or permit the slow undoing of those human rights to which this nation has always been committed, and to which we are committed today, at home and around the world."

"Let every nation know, whether it wishes us well or ill, that we shall pay any price, bear any burden, meet any hardship, support any friend, oppose any foe to assure the survival and the success of liberty."

"Let us never negotiate out of fear, but let us never fear to negotiate."

"All this will not be finished in the first one hundred days. Nor will it be finished in the first one thousand days, nor in the life of this administration, nor even perhaps in our lifetime on this planet. But let us begin."

"I do not believe that any of us would exchange places with any other people or any other generation. The energy, the faith, the devotion which we bring to this endeavor will light our country and all who serve it—and the glow from that fire can truly light the world."

"Now the trumpet summons us again—not as a call to bear arms, though arms we need—not as a call to battle, though embattled we are—but a call to bear the burden of a long twilight struggle, year in and year out, "rejoicing in hope, patient in tribulation"* —a struggle against the common enemies of man: tyranny, poverty, disease and war itself."

"My fellow citizens of the world: ask not what America will do for you, but what together we can do for the freedom of man."

---
*
Romans 12:12

The Inauguration

President Kennedy

66"Each president…is the president not only of all who live, but in a very real sense, of all those who have yet to live.

"The president's responsibility cannot be delegated. For he is the one focal point of responsibility. His office is the single channel through which there flow the torrential pressures and needs of every state, every federal agency, every friend and foe."

"To govern is to choose."

"On the presidential coat of arms, the American eagle holds in his right talon the olive branch, while in his left he holds a bundle of arrows. We intend to give equal attention to both."

"The president cannot afford–for the sake of the office as well as the nation–to be another Warren G. Harding, described by one backer as a man who 'would when elected, sign whatever bill the Senate sent him–and not send bills for the Senate to pass'; rather he must know when to lead the Congress, when to consult it, and when he should act alone."

"There are times when it is far better to do the right thing as a result of debate and sacrifice than the wrong thing as a testimonial to national unity."

"The unity of freedom has never relied on uniformity of opinion."

"Roosevelt fulfilled the role of moral leadership. So did Wilson and Lincoln, Truman and Jackson and Teddy Roosevelt. They led the people as well as the government–they fought for great ideals as well as bills."

"No one has a right to grade a president–not even poor James Buchanan–who has not sat in

President Kennedy

his chair, examined the mail and information that came across his desk, and learned why he made decisions."

Kennedy was reluctant to give assessments of himself or his presidency, answering such queries simply: "I have a nice home, the office is close by, and the pay is good."

After he'd been in office for a few months, he noted, "The only thing that really surprised us when we got into office was that things were just as bad as we had been saying they were; otherwise, we have been enjoying it very much."

"If anyone is crazy enough to want to kill a president of the United States, he can do it. All he must be prepared to do is give his life for the president's."

48   In his second State of the Union address to Congress on January 11, 1962, Kennedy said of his administration:

"The policy of this administration is to give to the individual the opportunity to realize his own highest possibilities."

"For it is the fate of this generation—of you in the Congress and of me as president—to live with a struggle we did not start, in a world we did not make. But the pressures of life are not always distributed by choice. And while no nation has ever faced such a challenge, no nation has ever been so ready to seize the burden and the glory of freedom."

In his third and ultimately final State of the Union address in 1963, Kennedy rejoiced in the nation's progress but urged Americans to prepare for the future:

"In short, both at home and abroad, there may now be a temptation to relax. For the road has been long, the burden heavy, and the pace consistently urgent. But we cannot be satisfied to rest here. This is the side of the hill, not the top. The mere absence of war is not peace. The mere absence of recession is not growth. We have made a beginning—but we have only begun. Now the time has come to make the most of our gains—to translate the renewal of our national strength into the achievement of our national purpose."

He looked back proudly and looked ahead with optimism:

"We are not lulled by the momentary calm of the sea or the somewhat clearer skies above. We know the turbulence that lies below, and the storms that are beyond the horizon this year. But now the winds of change appear to be blowing more strongly than ever, in the world of communism as well as our own. For 175 years we have sailed with those winds at our back, and with the tides of human freedom in our favor. We steer our ship with hope, as Thomas

Jefferson said, 'leaving Fear astern.' Today we still welcome those winds of change—and we have every reason to believe that our tide is running strong. With thanks to Almighty God for seeing us through a perilous passage, we ask His help anew in guiding the 'Good Ship Union.'"

President Kennedy

World Affairs

───── *The Role of the United States* ─────

"Experience has taught us that no one nation has the power or the wisdom to solve all the problems of the world or manage its revolutionary tides–that extending our commitments does not always increase our security–that any initiative carries with it the risk of a temporary defeat–that nuclear weapons cannot prevent subversion–that no free people can be kept free without will and energy of their own–and that no two nations or situations are exactly alike."

"Acting on our own, by ourselves, we cannot establish justice throughout the world; we cannot insure its domestic tranquillity, or provide for its common defense, or promote its general welfare, or secure the blessings of liberty to ourselves and our posterity. But joined with other free nations, we can do all this and more. We can assist the developing nations to throw off the yoke of poverty. We can balance our worldwide trade and payments at the highest possible level of growth. We can mount a deterrent powerful enough to deter any aggression. And ultimately we can help to achieve a world of law and free choice, banishing the world of war and coercion."

"Unless we are willing to take the leadership in the United States, next week as well as next year, unless we are willing to channel more of our ideas and our programs and delegate power to that body in the fight for peace, then we may expect to see the last great hope of peace swallowed up in the oceans of indifference and hate."

"We are a great revolutionary power, a great modern revolutionary country, which believes in the most progressive concepts which any country has ever been able to develop. Why should we look pallid and tired, while the Soviet Union, whose system of government is hostile to all the aspirations of human personality, should look progressive, and new and attract the intelligentsia and the students?"

"To renounce the world of freedom now, to abandon those who share our commitment, and retire into lonely and not so splendid isolation, would be to give communism the one hope which, in this twilight of disappointment for them, might repair their divisions and rekindle their hope."

"The great struggle in the world today is not one of popularity but one of power, and our power depends in considerable measure upon our ability to influence other nations, upon their willingness to associate themselves with our efforts, upon the strength of our stature and leadership."

"The single most important task of American foreign policy today is how we meet the challenge of imperialism, what we do to further man's desire to be free."

"Our historic task in this embattled age is not merely to defend freedom. It is to extend its writ and strengthen its covenant."

"In the long history of the world, only a few generations have been granted the role of defending freedom in its hour of maximum danger. I do not shrink from this responsibility- I welcome it."

In a message to Congress in May 1961, Kennedy remarked,

"These are extraordinary times. And we face an extraordinary challenge. Our strength as well as our convictions have imposed upon this nation the role of leader in freedom's cause. No role in history could be more difficult or more important. We stand for freedom."

"Let all our neighbors know that we shall join with them to oppose aggression or subversion anywhere in the Americas. And let every other power know that this hemisphere intends to remain the master of its own house."

"The fundamental task of our foreign aid program in the 1960s is not negatively to fight communism: its fundamental task is to help make a historical demonstration that, in

the twentieth century, as in the nineteenth…
economic growth and political democracy can
develop hand in hand."

"There are risks and costs to action. But
they are far less than the long-range risks of
comfortable inaction."

"Domestic policy can only defeat us; foreign
policy can kill us."

"The reason that Woodrow Wilson and
Franklin Roosevelt and Harry Truman were so
effective in their foreign policy was because they
were effective in their domestic policy, because
they were building a better country here."

President Kennedy spoke on foreign policy
at the University of Washington's 100th
Anniversary Program on November 16, 1961:
"We increase our arms at a heavy cost,
primarily to make certain that we will not have
to use them. We must face up to the chance of
war, if we are to maintain the peace."

"Through hot wars and cold, through recession and prosperity, through the ages of the atom and outer space, the American people have never faltered and their faith has never flagged. If at times our actions seem to make life difficult for others, it is only because history has made life difficult for us all."

"Let us see if we, in our own time, can move the world to a just and lasting peace. The effort to improve the conditions of man, however, is not a task for the few. It is the task of all nations, acting alone, acting in groups, acting in the United Nations; for plague and pestilence, and plunder and pollution, the hazards of nature and the hunger of children, are the foes of every nation. And science, technology, and education can be the allies of every nation."

President Kennedy spoke at the University of California at Berkeley in March 1962, presenting his vision of effective foreign policy: "The purpose of our aid programs must be to help developing countries to move forward as rapidly as possible on the road to genuine national independence. Our military policies must assist nations to protect the processes of democratic reform and development against the forces of disruption and intervention. Our diplomatic policies must strengthen our relations with the whole world, with our several alliances and within the United Nations."

"If we cannot end now our differences, at least we can help make the world safe for democracy."

"There used to be so much talk a few years ago about the inevitable triumph of communism. We hear such talk much less now. No one who examines the modern world can doubt that the great currents of history are carrying the world away from the monolithic idea toward the pluralistic idea–away from communism and toward national independence and freedom. No one can doubt that the wave of the future is not the conquest of the world by a single dogmatic creed but the liberation of the diverse energies of free nations and free men. No one can doubt that cooperation in the pursuit of knowledge must lead to freedom of the mind and freedom of the soul."

"Khrushchev reminds me of the tiger hunter who has picked a place on the wall to hang the tiger's skin long before he has caught the tiger. This tiger has other ideas."

"Some may choose forms and ways that we would not choose for ourselves—but it is not for us that they are choosing. We can welcome diversity—the Communists cannot. For we offer a world of choice—they offer the world of coercion."

"Though Mr. Khrushchev may claim that his nation, like ours, is also a home of the brave, this nation—not Russia—is still the land of the free."

"No government or social system is so evil that its people must be considered as lacking in virtue."

"If we are moving ahead, if we are demonstrating the vitality of our society, if the Communist system, which is as old as Egypt, looks as if it is moving ahead, and we look like we are standing still, then quite obviously those people will decide that the future belongs to them and not to us."

"Communism has sometimes succeeded as a scavenger but never as a leader. Communism has never come to power in a country that was not disrupted by war or corruption, or both."

"If freedom and communism were to compete for man's allegiance in a world at peace, I would look to the future with ever-increasing confidence."

"Peace need not be impracticable, and war need not be inevitable."

"The long labor of peace is an undertaking for every nation, and in this effort none of us can remain unaligned. To this goal none can be uncommitted."

"Peace is not solely a matter of military or technical problems; it is primarily a problem of politics and people. And unless man can match his strides in weaponry and technology with equal strides in social and political development, our great strength, like that of the dinosaur, will become incapable of proper control–and like the dinosaur vanish from the earth."

"Peace requires an America standing shoulder to shoulder with other free nations, united by close ties of commerce, friendship, and mutual respect. Americans cannot stand alone as a tiny minority in a hostile world, without friends and allies, without international effort to stem aggression from any source."

64   "Our aspiration is for peace, not merely a peace which lasts between wars, not merely a peace which hangs on the brink of war, not merely a peace of the death, but a peace enforced and controlled by the United Nations against the universal danger of common destruction. We want a peace in which the funds now poured into the destructive implements of war may be channeled into the constructive results of disarmament, in a great multinational effort to harness our rivers, eradicate disease, take care of our children, care for the aged. We want a peace in which we can truly beat our swords into plowshares, and our hydrogen bombs into atomic reactors."

"What kind of peace do I mean? What kind of peace do we seek? Not a Pax Americana enforced on the world by American weapons of war. Not the peace of the grave or the security of the slave. I am talking about genuine peace, the kind of peace that makes life on earth worth living, the kind that enables men and nations to grow and to hope and to build a better life for their children—not merely peace for Americans but peace for all men and women—not merely peace in our time but peace for all time."

"Let us examine our attitude toward peace itself. Too many of us think it is impossible. Too many think it unreal. But that is a dangerous, defeatist belief. It leads to the conclusion that war is inevitable—that mankind is doomed—that we are gripped by forces we cannot control."

Kennedy spoke on world peace at the United Nations in September 1963.

"Peace is a daily, a weekly, a monthly process, gradually changing opinions, slowly eroding old barriers, quietly building new structures. And however undramatic the pursuit of peace, that pursuit must go on."

"Peace is the necessary precondition for the advance of freedom...."

The Uncommon Wisdom of John F. Kennedy

"But peace does not rest in the charters and covenants alone. It lies in the hearts and minds of all people. So let us not rest all our hopes on parchment and on paper, let us strive to build peace, a desire for peace, a willingness to work for peace in the hearts and minds of all of our people. I believe that we can. I believe the problems of human destiny are not beyond the reach of human beings."

"Let us call a truce to terror. Let us invoke the blessings of peace. And, as we build an international capacity to keep peace, let us join in dismantling the national capacity to wage war."

"In this age of jets and atoms, we can no longer put our faith in war as a method of settling international disputes. We can no longer tolerate a world which is like a frontier town, without a sheriff or a magistrate."

"Total war makes no sense in an age when great powers can maintain large and relatively invulnerable nuclear forces and refuse to surrender without resort to those forces. It makes no sense in an age when a single nuclear weapon contains almost ten times the explosive force delivered by all the allied air forces in the Second World War. It makes no sense in an age when the deadly poisons produced by a nuclear exchange would be carried by wind and water and soil and seed to the far corners of the globe and to generations yet unborn."

"Unconditional war can no longer lead to unconditional victory. It can no longer serve to settle disputes. It can no longer concern the great powers alone. For a nuclear disaster, spread by wind and water and fear, could well engulf the great and the small, the rich and the poor, the committed and the uncommitted alike."

"The United States, as the world knows, will never start a war. We do not want a war. We do not now expect a war. This generation of Americans has already had enough—more than enough—of war and hate and oppression. We shall be prepared if others wish it. We shall be alert to try to stop it. But we shall also do our part to build a world of peace where the weak are safe and the strong are just."

"If we all can persevere, if we can in every land and office look beyond our own shores and ambitions, then surely the age will dawn in which the strong are just and the weak secure and the peace preserved."

"We seek not the worldwide victory of one nation or system but a worldwide victory of man."

"Those who make peaceful revolution impossible will make violent revolution inevitable."

"So long as fanaticism and fear brood over the affairs of men, we must arm to deter others from aggression."

"Any potential aggressor contemplating an attack on any part of the free world with any kind of weapons, conventional or nuclear, must know that our response will be suitable, selective, swift, and effective."

From an address to the General Assembly of the United Nations in 1961:

"We prefer world law in the age of self-determination to world war in the age of mass extermination."

"Mankind must put an end to war, or war will put an end to mankind."

"Freedom is indivisible, and when one man is enslaved, all are not free."

"The best road to progress is freedom's road."

"The very word 'secrecy' is repugnant in a free and open society; and we are as a people inherently and historically opposed to secret societies, to secret oaths, and to secret proceedings."

"What does truth require? It requires us to face the facts as they are, not to involve ourselves in self-deception; to refuse to think merely in slogans....What does justice require? In the end, it requires liberty."

"The truth doesn't die. The desire for liberty cannot be fully suppressed."

In a message to the Inter-American Economic and Social Conference at Punta del Este, Uruguay, in August 1961, Kennedy said, "Freedom is not merely a word or an abstract theory, but the most effective instrument for advancing the welfare of man."

"The great battleground for the defense and expansion of freedom today is the whole southern half of the globe . . . the lands of the rising peoples. Their revolution is the greatest in human history. They seek an end to injustice, tyranny and exploitation. More than an end, they seek a beginning."

On July 4, 1962, Kennedy spoke at Independence Hall in Philadelphia:

"The theory of independence is as old as man himself, and it was not invented in this hall. But it was in this hall that the theory became a practice; that the word went out to all, in Thomas Jefferson's phrase, that 'the God who gave us life, gave us liberty at the same time.' And today this nation–conceived in revolution, nurtured in liberty, maturing in independence–

has no intention of abdicating its leadership in that worldwide movement for independence to any nation or society committed to systematic human oppression."

"As apt and applicable as the Declaration of Independence is today, we would do well to honor that other historic document drafted in this hall–the Constitution of the United States. For it stressed not independence but interdependence–not the individual liberty of one but the indivisible liberty of all."

"To read [the Declaration of Independence] today is to hear a trumpet call. For that Declaration unleashed not merely a revolution against the British, but a revolution in human affairs."

66"**D**iplomacy and defense are not substitutes for one another. Either alone would fail."

"No one should be under the illusion that negotiations for the sake of negotiations always advance the cause of peace. But, while we shall negotiate freely, we shall not negotiate freedom. Our answer to the classic question of Patrick Henry is still 'No'—life is not so dear, and peace is not so precious, 'as to be purchased at the price of chains and slavery.' And that is our answer even though, for the first time since the ancient battles between Greek city-states, war entails the threat of total annihilation, of everything we know, of society itself. For to save mankind's future freedom, we must face up to any risk that is necessary. We will always seek peace—but we will never surrender."

Speaking on the establishment of the West

German Peace Corps in Bonn on June 24, 1963, Kennedy said of neutrality: "Dante once said that the hottest places in hell are reserved for those who in a period of moral crisis maintain their neutrality."

66**M**en may no longer pretend that the quest for disarmament is a sign of weakness—for in a spiraling arms race, a nation's security may well be shrinking even as its arms increase."

"To destroy arms, however, is not enough. We must create even as we destroy—creating worldwide law and law enforcement as we outlaw worldwide war and weapons."

"Today every inhabitant of this planet must contemplate that day when this planet may no longer be habitable. Every man, woman, and child lives under a nuclear sword of Damocles, hanging by the slenderest of threads, capable of being cut at any moment by accident or miscalculation or madness. The weapons of war must be abolished before they abolish us."

On July 26, 1963, Kennedy addressed the

American people regarding the Limited Test Ban Treaty and asked for their support and help in ensuring Senate approval.

"Each increase of tension has produced an increase of arms; each increase of arms has produced an increase of tension."

"A war today or tomorrow, if it led to nuclear war, would not be like any war in history. A full-scale nuclear exchange, lasting less than sixty minutes, with the weapons now in existence, could wipe out more than 300 million Americans, Europeans, and Russians, as well as untold numbers elsewhere. And the survivors, as Chairman Khrushchev warned the Communist Chinese, 'the survivors would envy the dead.' For they would inherit a world so devastated by explosion and poison and fire that today we cannot even conceive of its horrors. So let us try to turn the world away from war. Let us make the most of this opportunity, and every opportunity, to reduce tension, to slow down the perilous nuclear arms race, and to check the world's slide toward final annihilation."

"The loss of even one human life, or the malformation of even one baby—who may be born long after all of us have gone—should be of concern to us all."

"But now, for the first time in many years, the path of peace may be open. No one can be certain what the future will bring. No one can say whether the time has come for an easing of the struggle. But history and our own conscience will judge us harsher if we do not now make every effort to test our hopes by action, and this is the place to begin. According to the ancient Chinese proverb, 'A journey of a thousand miles must begin with a single step.' My fellow Americans, let us take that first step. Let us, if we can, step back from the shadows of war and seek out the way of peace. And if that journey is a thousand miles, or even more, let history record that we, in this land, at this time, took the first step."

The Limited Test Ban Treaty received a favorable Senate vote of 80 to 19 and went into effect in October 1963.

78 Asked how he became a war hero. Kennedy answered, "It was involuntary. They sank my boat."

"A young man who does not have what it takes to perform military service is not likely to have what it takes to make a living."

In a press conference on March 21, 1962, Kennedy spoke on military service: "There is always inequity in life. Some men are killed in a war and some men are wounded, and some men never leave the country.... Life is unfair."

"Since this country was founded, each generation of Americans has been summoned to give testimony to its national loyalty. The graves of young Americans who answered the call to service surround the globe."

On December 31, 1961, President Kennedy shared a message with members of the United States Armed Forces serving overseas, which was broadcast over Armed Forces radio networks:

"Our foreign policy is based on goals of freedom and justice. It is in the interest of these goals that we ask you to serve your country overseas. Your nation depends on you and your colleagues, not just for the execution of American foreign policy, but for the embodiment of the spirit and ideals of our country."

"There is an old story which I will close with which will give you very valuable advice as you follow a naval career—about a young yeoman who watched a lieutenant begin a meteoric career in the Navy, and he always used to go into his office every morning and go to his drawer and take out a piece of paper and look at it. He became the youngest captain, the youngest admiral, the youngest commander in chief. Finally one day he had a heart attack. The yeoman said, 'I want to see what is in that paper. It might help me.' So he went over and opened up the safe and pulled out the paper. And it said, 'Left—port; right—starboard.' "

66**A**rms alone are not enough to keep the peace–it must be kept by men. Our instrument and our hope is the United Nations– and I see little merit in the impatience of those who would abandon this imperfect world instrument because they dislike our imperfect world. For the troubles of a world organization merely reflect the troubles of the world itself. And if the organization is weakened, these troubles can only increase. We may not always agree with every detailed action taken by every officer of the United Nations, or with every voting majority. But as an institution, it should have in the future, as it has had in the past since its inception, no stronger or more faithful member than the United States of America."

"Today the United Nations is primarily the protector of the small and the weak, and a safety valve for the strong. Tomorrow it can form the framework for a world of law—a world in which no nation dictates the destiny of another, and in which the vast resources now devoted to destructive means will serve constructive ends."

"I don't think, really, in any sense, the United Nations has failed as a concept. I think occasionally we fail it."

"Never have the nations of the world had so much to lose or so much to gain. Together we shall save the planet or together we shall perish in its flames."

In September 1961, Kennedy spoke to the United Nations: "Until all the powerful are just, the weak will be secure only in the strength of this Assembly."

"The great question . . . is still before us: whether man's cherished hopes for progress and freedom are to be destroyed by terror and disruption; whether the 'four winds of war' can be tamed in time to free the cooling winds of reason; and whether the pledges of our Charter are to be fulfilled or defended—pledges to secure peace, progress, human rights, and world law."

"[The United Nations] will either grow to meet the challenge of our age, or it will be gone with the wind, without influence, without force, without respect. Were we to let it die, to enfeeble its vigor, to cripple its power, we would condemn the future."

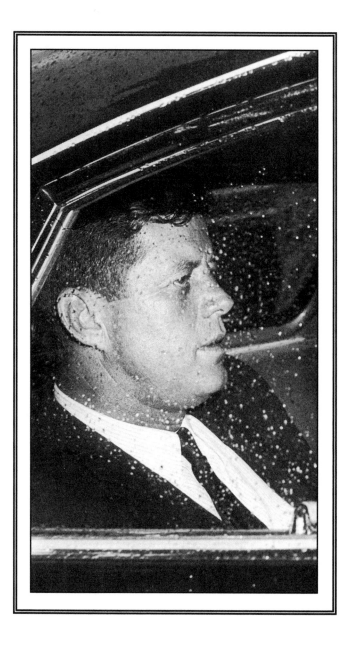

Kennedy in Trouble

The Bay of Pigs

President Kennedy's early anticommunism efforts focused on Cuban leader Fidel Castro. Shortly after Kennedy's inauguration, a group of CIA-trained anti-Castro Cuban exiles invaded Cuba in an attempt to overthrow the regime of Fidel Castro. Despite warnings from some advisers that covering up such a large-scale operation could backfire, Kennedy was intent on keeping the mission a secret in order to better ensure success.

Before the invasion, U.S. B-26 bombers attacked a number of Cuban airfields and planes. At the United Nations, Ambassador Adlai Stevenson, unaware of the secret operation, denied accusations by Cuba's Minister of Foreign Affairs of United States involvement. Photographs later revealed that the planes used in the attack were not from the Cuban Air Force, but from the U.S. The secret had been discovered.

Soviet leader Nikita Khrushchev wrote to President Kennedy, "It is a secret to no one that the armed bands invading this country were trained, equipped and armed in the United States of America. The planes which are bombing Cuban cities belong to the United States of America; the bombs they are dropping are being supplied by the American government."

After learning of U.S. involvement, Cuba responded immediately, sinking the command vessel *Maropa* and the supply ship *Houston*, which housed vital communication equipment and ammunition. Lacking supplies and promised air cover, 200 rebel soldiers were killed, 1,197 were captured, and four American pilots were killed. As a result of the incident, Kennedy fired longtime CIA Director Allen W. Dulles, Deputy Director Charles P. Cabell, and Deputy Director Richard Bissell and ordered an investigation of the operation.

Reflecting on this major embarrassment and foreign policy failure–"the perfect failure," as some called it–Kennedy said, "This was a struggle of Cuban patriots against a Cuban dictator."

On April 20, 1961, Kennedy addressed the American Society of Newspaper Editors to explain the invasion to the American people:

"We dare not fail to see the insidious nature of this new and deeper struggle. We dare not fail to grasp the new concepts, the new tools, the new sense of urgency we will need to combat it–whether in Cuba or South Vietnam. And we dare not fail to realize that this struggle is taking place every day, without fanfare, in thousands of villages and markets–day and night–and in classrooms all over the globe."

"Too long we have fixed our eyes on traditional military needs, on armies prepared to cross borders, on missiles poised for flight. Now it should be clear that this is no longer enough–that our security may be lost piece by piece, country by country, without the firing of a single missile or the crossing of a single border."

On April 21, 1961, while discussing the Bay of Pigs invasion, Kennedy told journalist Sander Vanocur: "Victory has a hundred fathers and defeat is an orphan."

In October 1962, the CIA secured intelligence photos detailing the Soviet Union's installation of nuclear missiles in Cuba, just ninety miles off the coast of Florida. Kennedy responded by blocking the delivery of all Soviet offensive weapons bound for Cuba. With the two mighty nations on the brink of nuclear war, the Soviets backed down and agreed to return the missiles to Russia. This agreement helped save the world from possible nuclear war.

On October 22, 1962, Kennedy gave a televised report to the American people on the Soviet arms buildup in Cuba:

"We will not act prematurely or unnecessarily risk the costs of worldwide nuclear war in which even the fruits of victory would be ashes in our mouth. But neither will we shrink from that risk at any time it must be faced."

"The 1930s taught us a clear lesson: aggressive conduct, if allowed to go unchecked and unchallenged, ultimately leads to war. This nation is opposed to war. We are also true to our word. Our unswerving objective, therefore, must be to prevent the use of these missiles against this or any other country, and to secure their withdrawal or elimination from the Western hemisphere."

"The path we have chosen for the present is full of hazards, as all paths are—but it is the one most consistent with our character and courage as a nation and our commitments around the world. The cost of freedom is always high—and Americans have always paid it. And one path we shall never choose, and that is the path of surrender or submission. Our goal is not the victory of might, but the vindication of right—not peace at the expense of freedom, but both peace and freedom, here in this hemisphere, and, we hope, around the world. God willing, that goal will be achieved."

At the height of the crisis, Kennedy remarked, "I guess this is the week I earn my salary."

Many presidents have only one major crisis during their times in office. John F. Kennedy had several in his short tenure as president, and the Berlin Crisis was in some ways the most significant. Kennedy had to walk a razor-thin line between preserving freedom and preventing war. One misstep could have provoked World War III. The Berlin Crisis demonstrates Kennedy's skill in dealing with foreign policy crises.

"The world is not deceived by the Communist attempt to label Berlin as a hotbed of war. There is peace in Berlin today. The source of world trouble and tension is Moscow, not Berlin. And if war begins, it will have begun in Moscow and not Berlin."

"We do not want to fight—but we have fought before. Those who threaten to unleash the forces of war on a dispute over West Berlin should recall the words of the ancient philosopher: 'A man who causes fear cannot be free from fear.' "

"I am well aware of the fact that many American families will bear the burden of these requests. Studies or careers will be interrupted; husbands and sons will be called away; incomes in some cases will be reduced. But these are burdens which must be borne if freedom is to be defended. Americans have willingly borne them before–and they will not flinch from the task now."

"I must emphasize again that the choice is not merely between resistance and retreat, between atomic holocaust and surrender. Our peacetime military posture is traditionally defensive; but our diplomatic posture need not be. Our response to the Berlin Crisis will not be merely military or negative. It will be more than merely standing firm. For we do not intend to leave it to others to choose and monopolize the forum and the framework of discussion. We do not intend to abandon our duty to mankind to seek a peaceful solution."

At City Hall in West Berlin, on June 26, 1963, Kennedy delivered one of his most famous speeches:

"There are many people in the world who really don't understand, or say they don't, what is the great issue between the free world and the Communist world. Let them come to Berlin. There are some who say that communism is the wave of the future. Let them come to Berlin. And there are some who say in Europe and elsewhere we can work with the Communists. Let them come to Berlin. And there are even a few who say that it is true that communism is an evil system, but it permits us to make economic progress. *Lass' sie nach Berlin kommen.* Let them come to Berlin."

"All free men, wherever they may live, are citizens of Berlin. And therefore, as a free man, I take pride in the words *'Ich bin ein Berliner.'* "

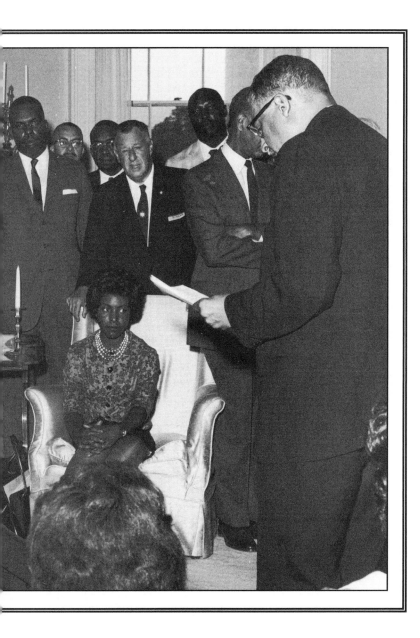

The National Agenda

The Economy

A strong economy was a major theme of Kennedy's second State of the Union address to Congress on January 11, 1962:

"When the youngest child alive today has grown to the cares of manhood, our position in the world will be determined first of all by what provisions we make today–for his education, his health, and his opportunities for a good home and a good job and a good life."

In his final State of the Union address to Congress in January 1963, Kennedy said:

"We shall be judged more by what we do at home than by what we preach abroad. Nothing we could do to help the developing countries would help them half as much as a booming U.S.

economy. And nothing our opponents could do to encourage their own ambitions would encourage them half as much as a chronic lagging U.S. economy. These domestic tasks do not divert energy from our security–they provide the very foundation for freedom's survival and success."

"It is increasingly clear that no matter what party is in power, so long as our national security needs keep rising, an economy hampered by restrictive tax rates will never produce enough jobs or enough profits."

"If a free society cannot help the many who are poor, it cannot save the few who are rich."

"I believe in an America where every man or woman who wants to find work can find work– where a growing economy provides new jobs and new markets for a growing nation without inflating the consumer's prices beyond the reach of his family budget."

"Our primary challenge is not how to divide the economic pie, but how to enlarge it."

"If men have the talent to invent new machines that put men out of work, they have the talent to put those men back to work."

On economic preparedness: "The time to repair the roof is when the sun is shining."

Speaking in Pueblo, Colorado, on August 17, 1962, Kennedy said of economic progress: "A rising tide lifts all the boats."

"The farmer is the only man in our economy who buys everything at retail, sells everything he produces at wholesale, and pays the freight both ways."

Four days before his death, Kennedy spoke to the Inter-American Press Association in Miami Beach:

"[The] hope [for the future] is for a hemisphere where every man has enough to eat and a chance to work, where every child can learn and every family can find decent shelter. It is for a hemisphere where every man, from the

American Negro to the Indian of the Altiplano, can be liberated from the bonds of social injustice, free to pursue his own talents as far as they will take him, allowed to participate in the fruits of progress."

President Kennedy made great advances in the civil rights movement during his time in office. Recognizing the movement as a vital cause early on, his devotion to civil rights while in office led to several milestones in the fight for equality.

"One hundred years have passed since President Lincoln freed the slaves, yet their heirs, their grandsons, are not fully free. They are not yet freed from the bonds of injustice. They are not yet freed from social and economic oppression. And this nation, for all its hopes and all its boasts, will not be fully free until all its citizens are free."

"No one can deny the complexity of the problems involved in assuring to all of our citizens their full rights as Americans. But no one can gainsay the fact that the determination to secure these rights is in the highest traditions of American freedom."

"Irrational barriers and ancient prejudices fall quickly when the question of survival itself is at stake."

"If we cannot end now our differences, at least we can help make the world safe for diversity."

"No one has been barred on account of his race from fighting or dying for America—there are no 'white' or 'colored' signs on the foxholes or graveyards of battle."

"What we are seeking, after all, is really very simple. It's merely a recognition that this is one nation and we are all one great people. Our origins may be different but our destiny is the same, our aspirations are identical. There can be no artificial distinctions, no arbitrary barriers, in securing these rights. The right of every man to work as he wants to work, to be educated as every human being deserves to be educated, and to receive for his labor or his crops or his goods a just compensation, which he can spend as he pleases, in the nation's finest luxury store or the most modest five-and-ten. The right of every family to live in a decent home in a decent neighborhood of his own free choice. The right of every individual to obtain security in sickness as well as health, in retirement as well as youth. The right of every American to think, to vote, to speak, to read, and to worship as he pleases—to stand up for his rights and, when necessary, to sit down for them. And finally, the right of all people to be free from the tensions and terrors and burdens of war, its preparation and its consequences....Our job is to turn the American vision of a society in which no man has to suffer discrimination based on race into a living reality everywhere in our land."

"A strong America cannot neglect the aspirations of its citizens—the welfare of the needy, the health care of the elderly, the education of the young. For we are not developing the nation's wealth for its own sake. Wealth is the means—and people are the ends. All our material riches will avail us little if we do not use them to expand the opportunities of our people."

Addressing students at East Los Angeles College in November 1960, Kennedy spoke on civil rights and equal employment: "We do not want a Negro who could be a doctor, in a city short of doctors, working as a messenger."

On equal voting rights: "I wish that all qualified Americans permitted to vote were willing to vote, but surely in this centennial year of Emancipation all those who are willing to vote should always be permitted."

In June 1963, the Alabama National Guard had to be called out to quell unrest on the University of Alabama campus, in reaction to the court-ordered admission of two black students. On June 11, Kennedy gave a televised report from the White House to the American people on the heated issue of civil rights:

"I hope that every American, regardless of where he lives, will stop and examine his conscience about this and other related incidents. This nation was founded by men of many nations and backgrounds. It was founded on the principle that all men are created equal, and that the rights of every man are diminished when the rights of one man are threatened."

"Today we are committed to a worldwide struggle to promote and protect the rights of all who wish to be free. And when Americans are sent to Vietnam or West Berlin, we do not ask for whites only. It ought to be possible, therefore, for American students of any color to attend any public institution they select without having to be backed up by troops."

"It ought to be possible for American consumers of any color to receive equal service in places of public accommodation, such as hotels and restaurants and theaters and retail stores, without being forced to resort to demonstrations in the street, and it ought to be possible for American citizens of any color to register to vote in a free election without interference or fear of reprisal. It ought to be possible, in short, for every American to enjoy the privileges of being American without regard to his race or his color. In short, every American ought to have the right to be treated as he would wish to be treated, as one would wish his children to be treated. But

this is not the case."

"We are confronted primarily with a moral issue. It is as old as the scriptures and is as clear as the American Constitution. The heart of the question is whether all Americans are to be afforded equal rights and equal opportunities, whether we are going to treat our fellow Americans as we want to be treated. If an American, because his skin is dark, cannot eat lunch in a restaurant open to the public, if he cannot send his children to the best public school available, if he cannot vote for the public officials who will represent him, if, in short, he cannot enjoy the full and free life which all of us want, then who among us would be content to have the color of his skin changed and stand in his place? Who among us would then be content with the counsels of patience and delay?"

"Now the time has come for this nation to fulfill its promise. The events in Birmingham and elsewhere have so increased the cries for equality that no city or state or legislative body can prudently choose to ignore them. The fires of frustration and discord are burning in every city, North and South, where legal remedies are not at hand. Redress is sought in the streets, in demonstrations, parades, and protests which create tensions and threaten violence and threaten lives. We face, therefore, a moral crisis as a country and as a people. It cannot be met by repressive police action. It cannot be left to increased demonstrations in the streets. It cannot be quieted by token moves or talk. It is a time to act in the Congress, in your state and local legislative body and, above all, in all of our daily lives. It is not enough to pin the blame on others, to say this is a problem of one section of the country or another, or deplore the fact that we face. A great change is at hand, and our task, our obligation, is to make that revolution, that change, peaceful and constructive for all. Those who do nothing are inviting shame as well as violence. Those who act boldly are recognizing right as well as reality."

"I ask you to look into your hearts—not in search of charity, for the Negro neither wants nor needs condescension—but for the one plain, proud and priceless quality that unites us all as Americans: a sense of justice. In this year of the Emancipation Centennial, justice requires us to insure the blessings of liberty for all Americans and their posterity—not merely for reasons of economic efficiency, world diplomacy and domestic tranquillity—but, above all, because it is right."

Kennedy fought throughout his career for improved education and the welfare of children.

"Our children and our grandchildren...have no lobby here in Washington.... [They] are not merely statistics toward which we can be indifferent."

"The genius of our scientists has given us the tools to bring abundance to our land, strength to our industry, and knowledge to our people. For the first time we have the capacity to strike off the remaining bonds of poverty and ignorance–to free our people for the spiritual and intellectual fulfillment which has always been the goal of our civilization."

"Not every child has an equal talent or an equal ability or an equal motivation, but they should have the equal right to develop their talent and their ability and their motivation, to make something of themselves."

"We must think and act not only for the moment but for the century. I am reminded of the story of the great French Marshal Lyautey, who once asked his gardener to plant a tree. The gardener objected that the tree was slow-growing and would not reach maturity for a hundred years. The Marshal replied, 'In that case, there is no time to lose, plant it this afternoon.' Today a world of knowledge—a world of cooperation—a just and lasting peace—may be years away. But we have no time to lose. Let us plant our trees this afternoon."

In remarks at Amherst College on October 26, 1963, Kennedy urged students to use their education for the good of the nation: "There is inherited wealth in this country and also inherited poverty. And unless the graduates of this college and other colleges like it who are given a running start in life—unless they are willing to put back into our society, those talents, the broad sympathy, the understanding, the compassion—unless they are willing to put those qualities back into the service of the Great Republic, then obviously the presuppositions upon which our democracy are based are bound to be fallible."

In his State of the Union address on January 11, 1962, Kennedy told members of Congress, " 'Civilization,' said H. G. Wells, 'is a race between education and catastrophe.' It is up to you in this Congress to determine the winner of that race."

"This nation cannot afford to maintain its military power and neglect its brainpower."

"Leadership and learning are indispensable to each other."

"Man is still the most extraordinary computer of all."

Speaking at Vanderbilt University in Nashville, Kennedy said:

"Liberty without learning is always in peril, and learning without liberty is always in vain."

During a 1962 address at the University of California at Berkeley, Kennedy told those gathered, "Knowledge, not hate, is the passkey to the future—that knowledge transcends national antagonisms—that it is the possession, not of a single class or of a single nation or a single ideology, but of all mankind."

"In a time of turbulence and change, it is more true than ever that knowledge is power."

"If...history...teaches us anything, it is that man, in his quest for knowledge and progress, is determined and cannot be deterred."

"We do not undertake to meet our growing educational problems merely to compare our achievements with those of our adversaries. These measures are justified on their own merits—in times of peace as well as peril, to educate better citizens as well as better scientists and soldiers."

Kennedy echoed the thoughts of playwright George Bernard Shaw in a speech delivered in Dublin, Ireland, in June 1963:

"Modern cynics and skeptics...see no harm in paying those to whom they entrust the minds of their children a smaller wage than is paid to those to whom they entrust the care of their plumbing."

From a speech about the importance of education at Vanderbilt University: "The ignorance of one voter in a democracy impairs the security of all."

Kennedy reassured the American people upon signing the Maternal and Child Health and Mental Retardation Planning Bill into law on October 24, 1963: "We can say with some assurance that, although children may be the victims of fate, they will not be the victims of our neglect."

In his final State of the Union address to Congress in January 1963, Kennedy urged Congress to improve overcrowded national parks and recreation areas: "If we do not plan today for the future growth of these and other great natural assets—not only parks and forests but wildlife and wilderness preserves, and water projects of all kinds—our children and their children will be poorer in every sense of the word."

Kennedy's commencement address at San Diego State College in June 1963 focused on education and civil rights:

"American children today do not yet enjoy equal educational opportunities for two primary reasons: One is economic and the other is racial. If our nation is to meet the goal of giving every American child a fair chance—because an uneducated child makes an uneducated parent who in another day produces another uneducated child—we must move ahead swiftly in both areas."

"The pursuit of knowledge itself implies a world where men are free to follow out the logic of their own ideas. It implies a world where nations are free to solve their own problems and to realize their own ideals. It implies, in short, a world where collaboration emerges from the voluntary decisions of nations strong in their own independence and their own self-respect. It implies, I believe, the kind of world which is emerging before our eyes–the world produced by the revolution of national independence which has today, and has been since 1945, sweeping across the face of the world."

On October 14, 1960, in the final weeks of his presidential campaign, Senator Kennedy planted the seeds for the Peace Corps to a young audience gathered at the Student Union building steps at the University of Michigan in Ann Arbor, Michigan:

"How many of you who are going to be doctors are willing to spend your days in Ghana? Technicians or engineers, how many of you are willing to work in the Foreign Service and spend your lives traveling around the world? On your willingness to do that, not merely to serve one year or two years in the service, but on your willingness to contribute part of your life to this country..."

In an address to the Delegates to the Youth Fitness Conference on February 21, 1961, Kennedy shared his early vision of the Peace

Corps with his young audience:

"The benefits of the Peace Corps will not be limited to the countries in which it serves. Our own young men and women will be enriched by the experience of living and working in foreign lands. They will have acquired new skills and experience which will aid them in their future careers and add to our own country's supply of trained personnel and teachers. They will return better able to assume the responsibilities of American citizenship and with greater understanding of our global responsibilities."

"Life in the Peace Corps will not be easy. There will be no salary and allowances will be at a level sufficient only to maintain health and meet basic needs. Men and women will be expected to work and live alongside the nationals of the country in which they are stationed–doing the same work, eating the same food, talking the same language. But if the life will not be easy, it will be rich and satisfying. For every young American who participates in the Peace Corps– who works in a foreign land–will know that he or she is sharing in the great common task of bringing to man that decent way of life which is the foundation of freedom and a condition of peace."

Kennedy praised both the national and international benefits of the Peace Corps in his final State of the Union address to Congress in January 1963: "In the end, the crucial effort is one of purpose, requiring the fuel of finance but also a torch of idealism. And nothing carries the spirit of this American idealism more effectively to the far corners of the earth than the American Peace Corps."

Since its founding in March 1961, more than 169,000 Americans have served in the Peace Corps in 136 nations.

E very child growing up in America in the 1960s knew John F. Kennedy's dream for space exploration: "I believe that this nation should commit itself to achieving the goal, before this decade is out, of landing a man on the moon and returning him safely to the earth." On July 20, 1969, Kennedy's dream was accomplished with the first moon landing.

"We choose to go to the moon. We choose to go to the moon in this decade and do the other things, not because they are easy, but because they are hard, because that goal will serve to organize and measure the best of our energies and skills, because that challenge is one that we are willing to accept, one we are unwilling to postpone, and one which we intend to win, and the others, too."

"Many years ago the great British explorer

George Mallory, who was to die on Mount Everest, was asked why did he want to climb it. He said, 'Because it is there.' Well, space is there, and we're going to climb it, and the moon and the planets are there, and new hopes for knowledge and peace are there. And, therefore, as we set sail we ask God's blessing on the most hazardous and dangerous and greatest adventure on which man has ever embarked."

Kennedy remarked during his 1962 address at the University of California at Berkeley:

"We may be proud as a nation of our record in scientific achievement—but at the same time we must be impressed by the interdependence of all knowledge. I am certain that every scholar and scientist here today would agree that his own work has benefited immeasurably from the work of the men and women in other countries. The prospect of a partnership with Soviet scientists in the exploration of space opens up exciting prospects of collaboration in other areas of learning. And cooperation in the pursuit of knowledge can hopefully lead to cooperation in the pursuit of peace."

During a campaign stop in Michigan in September 1960, Kennedy acknowledged Russian progress in space: "It is, I think, a source of concern to us that the first dogs carried around in outer space were not named Rover and Fido, but instead were named Belka and Strelka." Then, referring to his opponent Nixon's famous dog, "It was not named Checkers, either."

"The chimpanzee who is flying in space took off at 10:08. He reports that everything is perfect and working well."

Kennedy spoke at Rice University in Houston, Texas, on September 12, 1962, on America's bold new space exploration efforts:

"Those who came before us made certain that this country rode the first waves of the industrial revolutions, the first waves of modern invention, and the first wave of nuclear power, and this generation does not intend to founder in the backwash of the coming age of space. We mean to be a part of it—we mean to lead it.

For the eyes of the world now look into space, to the moon and to the planets beyond, and we have vowed that we shall not see it governed by a hostile flag of conquest, but by a banner of freedom and peace. We have vowed that we shall not see space filled with weapons of mass destruction, but with instruments of knowledge and understanding."

"We set sail on this new sea because there is new knowledge to be gained, and new rights to be won, and they must be won and used for the progress of all people. For space science, like nuclear science and all technology, has no conscience of its own. Whether it will become a force for good or ill depends on man, and only if the United States occupies a position of preeminence can we help decide whether this new ocean will be a sea of peace or a new terrifying theater of war."

"In a very real sense, it will not be one man going to the moon…it will be an entire nation. For all of us must work to put him there."

Kennedy noted enthusiastically at the dedication of the Aerospace Medical Health Center in San Antonio, Texas, on November 21, 1963: "This nation has tossed its cap over the wall of space, and we have no choice but to follow it."

"When we make a great national effort, to make sure that free men are not second in space, we move in the same direction that Thomas Jefferson moved in when he sent Lewis and Clark to the far reaches of this country during his term of office."

“We must never forget that art is not a form of propaganda; it is a form of truth.”

During Kennedy's presidency, the White House hosted many artistic and literary personalities—perhaps more than at any time in our history. Kennedy once joked, "It's becoming a sort of eating place for artists. But they never ask us out!"

"Too often in the past, we have thought of the artist as an idler and dilettante and of the lover of arts as somehow sissy and effete. We have done both an injustice. The life of the artist is, in relation to his work, stern and lonely. He has labored hard, often amid deprivation, to perfect his skill. He has turned aside from quick success in order to strip his vision of everything secondary or cheapening. His working life is marked by intense application and intense discipline."

"If sometimes our great artists have been the most critical of our society, it is because their sensitivity and their concern for justice, which must motivate any true artist, makes him aware that our nation falls short of its highest potential. I see little of more importance to the future of our country and our civilization than full recognition of the place of the artist."

"When power leads man toward arrogance, poetry reminds him of his limitations. When power narrows the area of man's concern, poetry reminds him of the richness and diversity of his existence. When power corrupts, poetry cleanses."

Speaking at Harvard in 1956, Kennedy stressed the importance of the arts: "The life of the arts, far from being an interruption, a distraction in the life of a nation, is very close to the center of a nation's purpose—and it is the test of the quality of a nation's civilization."

"The arts incarnate the creativity of a free people. When the creative impulse cannot flourish, when it cannot freely select its methods and objects, when it is deprived of spontaneity, then society severs the root of art."

"Art is the great democrat, calling forth creative genius from every sector of society, disregarding race or religions or wealth or color."

Kennedy appointed his favorite poet, Robert Frost, Poet Laureate of the U.S. Frost delivered one of his most famous poems, "The Gift Outright," at Kennedy's inauguration.[*]

In remarks recorded for a television tribute to Frost, broadcast over the Columbia Broadcasting System on February 26, 1961, Kennedy shared, "I asked Robert Frost to come and speak at the inauguration not merely because I was desirous of according a recognition to his trade, but also because I felt he had something important to say to those of us who are occupied with the business of government, that he would remind us that we were dealing with life, the hopes and fears of millions of people, and also to tell us that our own deep convictions must be the ultimate guide to all of our actions."

---

[*] Frost had originally planned to deliver a new poem written for the occasion, but the glare from the sun blinded him and forced him to deliver "The Gift Outright" from memory.

Kennedy issued a statement upon the death of Robert Frost on January 29, 1963.

"The death of Robert Frost leaves a vacancy in the American spirit. He was the great American poet of our time. His art and his life summed up the essential qualities of the New England he loved so much: the fresh delight in nature, the plainness of speech, the canny wisdom, and the deep, underlying insight into the human soul. His death impoverishes us all; but he has bequeathed his nation a body of imperishable verse from which Americans will forever gain joy and understanding. He had promises to keep, and miles to go, and now he sleeps."

"There are many kinds of courage—bravery under fire, courage to risk reputation and friendship and career for convictions which are deeply held. Perhaps the rarest courage of all for the skill to pursue it is given to very few men—is the courage to wage a silent battle to illuminate the nature of man and the world in which he lives. This is Robert Frost's courage."

"In serving his vision of the truth, the artist best serves his nation. And the nation which disdains the mission of art invites the fate of Robert Frost's 'hired man,' the fate of having 'nothing to look backward to with pride, and nothing to look forward to with hope.'"

"In free society art is not a weapon and it does not belong to the sphere of polemics and ideology. Artists are not engineers of the soul. It may be different elsewhere. But democratic society—in it, the highest duty of the writer, the composer, the artist, is to remain true to himself and to let the chips fall where they may."

Just two months after Kennedy's assassination, Congress designated the National Cultural Center, a product of the 1958 National Cultural Center Act, as a "living memorial" to President Kennedy. Twenty-three million dollars was authorized by Congress to help construct what is now known as the John F. Kennedy Center for the Performing Arts, on the banks of the Potomac River in Washington, D.C. It opened in September 1971.

The following words Kennedy spoke are inscribed at the John F. Kennedy Center for the

Performing Arts:

"There is a connection, hard to explain logically but easy to feel, between achievement in public life and progress in the arts. The age of Pericles was also the age of Phidias. The age of Lorenzo de Medici was also the age of Leonardo Da Vinci. The age of Elizabeth was also the age of Shakespeare, and the new frontier for which I campaign in American life can also be a new frontier for American art."

"I look forward to an America which will reward achievement in the arts as we reward achievement in business or statecraft. I look forward to an America which will steadily raise the standards of artistic accomplishment and which will steadily enlarge cultural opportunities for all of our citizens. And I look forward to an America which commands respect throughout the world not only for its strength, but for its civilization as well."

130 "The earth can be an abundant mother to all of the people that will be born in the coming years if we learn how to use her with skill and wisdom to heal her wounds, replenish her vitality, and utilize her potentialities.

"It is our task in our time and in our generation to hand down undiminished to those who come after us, as was handed down to us by those who went before, the natural wealth and beauty which is ours."

Though seemingly fit and athletic, Kennedy was in fact beset with a variety of physical ailments during his presidency, including severe back pain. Perhaps in part because of his own struggles, Kennedy stressed the vital importance of physical fitness to the nation:

"What we must do is literally change the physical habits of millions of Americans; and that is far more difficult than changing their tastes, their fashions, or even their politics."

"I think we ought to concern ourselves with making sure that our children are fit, that they are concerned with being energetic–that they use their young years not merely as spectators but as participants in life."

"We want to make sure that as our life becomes more sophisticated, as we become more urbanized, that we don't lose this very valuable facet of our national character: physical vitality, which is tied into qualities of character, which is tied into qualities of intellectual vigor and vitality."

Family, Religion, and the White House

Despite the pressures of his job, John F. Kennedy always found great comfort, refuge, and strength in his family and home. As president, his devotion to family was on display for the entire nation to see.

In September 1953, then-senator Kennedy married Jacqueline Bouvier. Jacqueline Bouvier Kennedy was perhaps the most glamorous and popular first lady in history. When she and her husband visited Paris in 1962, she spoke French fluently, enchanting everyone she met, including President Charles de Gaulle.

When the time came for Kennedy to bid his French hosts adieu at a press conference, he said, "I do not think it entirely inappropriate to introduce myself to this audience. I am the man who accompanied Jacqueline Kennedy to Paris, and I have enjoyed it."

On one of many trips with Jacqueline, Kennedy told an audience, "I appreciate you being here this morning. Mrs. Kennedy is organizing herself. It takes her longer, but, of course, she looks better than we do when she does it."

John and Jackie's first child, Caroline, was born in November 1957. Two months before his inauguration, on November 25, 1960, the president-elect and Jackie Kennedy welcomed their second child, John Jr.

Joseph Kennedy once remarked to his son John about his granddaughter Caroline, "She's very bright—smarter than you were, Jack, at that age."

"Yes, she is," Kennedy agreed, "but look who she has for a father!"

One afternoon during the Cuban Missile

Crisis, Kennedy saw his daughter lunging hyperactively across the White House lawn.

"Caroline!" he shouted to her. "Have you been eating candy?"

Caroline said nothing.

"Caroline, have you been eating candy? Answer yes, no, or maybe."

Because she was so candid and forthcoming, Caroline was a great favorite of the White House press camp. When one congressman told Kennedy that Caroline had told him that she didn't want to live in the White House anymore, Kennedy replied, "That's not my problem with Caroline," he said. "My problem is to keep her from holding press conferences."

During a speech at a state fair in West Virginia, Kennedy held up a toy donkey and said, "I have been presented with this donkey by two young ladies down there for my daughter. My daughter has the greatest collection of donkeys. She doesn't even know what an elephant looks like. We are going to protect her from that knowledge."

The appointment by Kennedy of his brother as attorney general raised some eyebrows. President Kennedy once joked with the press:

"I've been criticized by quite a few people for making my brother Bobby attorney general. They didn't realize that I had a very good reason for that appointment. Bobby wants to practice law, and I thought he ought to get a little experience first."

One magazine called Robert Kennedy "the man with the greatest influence at the White House." A few days later, Bobby phoned Jack, who put his hand over the receiver to tell a guest, "This is the second most powerful man in the nation calling."

During the long 1960 campaign for the presidency, the public had difficulty differentiating John and Robert Kennedy. Once, on a flight from Boston to Washington, John Kennedy was questioned by a woman seated next to him. "Aren't you afraid those terrible labor union racketeers will do something to your seven lovely children?"

Kennedy replied, "That's not me, that's my brother."

As the plane landed, the woman said, "Well, I hope your brother gets to be president."

"That's not my brother," Kennedy said. "That's me."

In an article in *Time* magazine in June 1962, Ted Kennedy, freshly nominated for a Senate seat, was described as smiling "sardonically." President Kennedy took exception to this, saying: "Bobby and I smile sardonically. Ted will learn how to smile sardonically in two or three years, but he doesn't know how yet."

That America would never elect a Catholic president was the prevailing wisdom in many political circles. John F. Kennedy proved these pundits wrong, and by doing so, opened the doors for others previously considered unelectable. Kennedy said it best when he spoke these words: "I am not the Catholic candidate for president. I am the Democratic Party's candidate for president, who happens also to be a Catholic."

Kennedy asked for voters to judge his experience and not his faith.

"I hope that no American, considering the really critical issues facing this country, will waste his franchise by voting either for me or against me solely on account of my religious affiliation. It is not relevant. I am telling you now what you are entitled to know: that my decisions on any public policy will be my own—as an American, a Democrat, and a free man.

"Are we going to admit to the world that a Jew can be elected mayor of Dublin, a Protestant can be chosen foreign minister in France, a Moslem can serve in the Israeli Parliament, but a Catholic cannot be elected president of the United States? .... Are we to admit to the world—worse still, are we to admit to ourselves—that one-third of our population is forever barred from the White House?"

"Nobody asked me if I was a Catholic when I joined the United States Navy."

"While they came from a wide variety of religious backgrounds and held a wide variety of religious beliefs, each of our presidents in his own way has placed a special trust in God. Those who were strongest intellectually were also strongest spiritually."

Kennedy frequently deflected the issue of his Catholicism with humor:

"The reporters are constantly asking me my views of the Pope's infallibility. And so I asked my friend Cardinal Spellman what I should say when reporters ask me whether I feel the Pope is infallible. And Cardinal Spellman said, 'I don't know what to tell you, Senator. All I know is that he keeps calling me 'Spillman.' ' "

From a letter Kennedy wrote in 1957:

"Never in my public life have I been approached by a representative of the Catholic Church or, for that matter, any other church, to perform an official act which was not consistent with the public interest as I saw it."

"The president is not elected to be protector of the faith—or guardian of the public morals. His attendance at church on Sunday should be his business alone, not a showcase for the nation."

"But because I am a Catholic, and no Catholic has ever been elected president, the real issues in this campaign have been obscured—perhaps deliberately, in some quarters less responsible than this. So it is apparently necessary for me to state once again–not what kind of church I believe in, for that should be important only to me–but what kind of America I believe in. I believe in an America where the separation of church and state is absolute–where no Catholic prelate would tell the president (should he be Catholic) how to act, and no Protestant minister would tell his parishioners for whom to vote– where no church or church school is granted any public funds or political preference–and where no man is denied public office merely because his religion differs from the president who might appoint him or the people who might elect him."

"Whatever issue may come before me as president–on birth control, divorce, censorship, gambling, or any other subject–I will make my decision in accordance with these views, in accordance with what my conscience tells me to be the national interest, and without regard to outside religious pressures or dictates. And no power or threat of punishment could cause me to decide otherwise. . . ."

The Uncommon Wisdom of John F. Kennedy

"I do not speak for my church on public matters—and the church does not speak for me."

Once, when he was asked whether he thought his religion would cost him any votes, Kennedy replied, "I feel as a Catholic that I'll get my reward in my life hereafter, although I may not get it here."

"If I should lose on the real issues, I shall return to my seat in the Senate, satisfied that I had tried my best and was fairly judged. But if this election is decided on the basis that 40 million Americans lost their chance of being president on the day they were baptized, then it is the whole nation that will be the loser, in the eyes of Catholics and non-Catholics around the world, in the eyes of history, and in the eyes of our own people."

Kennedy addressed the Houston Ministerial Association on September 12, 1960:

"I want to emphasize from the outset that we have far more critical issues to face in the 1960 election; the spread of Communist influence, until it now festers 90 miles off the coast of Florida–the humiliating treatment of our president and vice president by those who no longer respect our power–the hungry children I saw in West Virginia, the old people who cannot pay their doctor bills, the families forced to give up their farms–an America with too many slums, with too few schools, and too late to the moon and outer space. These are the real issues which should decide this campaign. And they are not religious issues–for war and hunger and ignorance and despair know no religious barriers."

When he heard that the Vatican had criticized his repeated statements that he would not be influenced by the Pope when it came to leading his country, Kennedy replied, "Now I understand why Henry the Eighth set up his own church!"

When he announced his opposition to federal aid for parochial schools, Kennedy received stern criticism from Catholic officials. After he formally proposed his education bill to Congress, he quipped, "As all of you know, some circles invented the myth that after Al Smith's defeat in 1928, he sent a one-word telegram to the Pope: 'Unpack.' After my press conference on the school bill, I received a one-word wire from the Pope: 'Pack.'"

"The guiding principle and prayer of this nation has been, is now, and shall ever be 'In God We Trust.'"

A fter the White House gardens had been
replanted with border flowers, ageratum,
and petunias, Kennedy strolled through, deeply
impressed by the gardeners' handiwork. "This
may go down as the real achievement of this
administration," he joked.

President Kennedy welcomed a group of
Fulbright exchange teachers from abroad to the
White House in August 1962. "I'm glad you've
seen something of the White House. It belongs
to all of the American people, and is also where
I live."

Speaking to Nobel Prize winners at a White
House reception, Kennedy remarked, "I think
this is the most extraordinary collection of
talent, of human knowledge, that has ever been
gathered together at the White House with the
possible exception of when Thomas Jefferson

dined here alone."

Upon moving into the White House, Kennedy sought to change the decor and make the building more accessible to the public. The first lady headed the redecoration efforts and led a televised tour of the White House in January 1962, to an audience of nearly 80 million viewers. Kennedy remarked, "I'd like to make this White House the living museum of the decorative arts in America."

On June 28, 1963, during a tour of Europe, Kennedy told a crowd in New Ross, Ireland, "About fifty years ago, an Irishman from New Ross traveled down to Washington with his family. And in order to tell his neighbors how well he was doing, he had his picture taken in front of the White House and said, 'This is our summer home. Come and see it.' "

Politics and the Press

66"**M**others all want their sons to grow up to be president, but they don't want them to become politicians in the process."

"My brother Bob doesn't want to be in government—he promised Dad he'd go straight," joked Kennedy.

"Those of you who regard my profession of political life with disdain should remember that it made it possible for me to move from being an obscure lieutenant in the United States Navy to commander in chief in fourteen years with very little technical competence."

"Politics is like football; if you see daylight, go through the hole."

"I have never taken the view that the world of politics and the world of poetry are so far apart. I think politicians and poets share at least one thing, and that is that their greatness depends upon the courage with which they face the challenges of life."

"No president, it seems to me, can escape politics. He has not only been chosen by the nation—he has been chosen by his party. And if he insists that he is 'president of all the people' and should, therefore, offend none of them—if he blurs the issues and differences between the parties—if he neglects the party machinery and avoids his party's leadership—then he has not only weakened the political party as an instrument of the democratic process—he has dealt a blow to the democratic process itself."

"No responsibility of government is more fundamental than the responsibility of maintaining the highest standards of ethical behavior by those who conduct the public business."

"There can be no dissent from the principle that all officials must act with unwavering integrity, absolute impartiality, and complete devotion to the public interest."

"Let us not seek the Republican answer or the Democratic answer but the right answer."

President Kennedy addressed a meeting of the Democratic National Committee on January 21, 1961.

"The party is not an end in itself–it is a means to an end.... The party is the means by which programs can be put into action–the means by which people of talent can come to the service of the country. And in this great free society of ours, both of our parties–the Republican and the Democratic parties–serve the interests of the people."

"Most of us are conditioned for many years to have a political viewpoint–Republican or Democratic, liberal, conservative, or moderate. The fact of the matter is that most of the problems...that we now face are technical problems, are administrative problems. They are very sophisticated judgments, which do not lend themselves to the great sort of passionate movements which have stirred this country so often in the past. [They] deal with questions which are now beyond the comprehension of most men."

Kennedy shared his thoughts on political party labels during the second Kennedy-Nixon presidential debate of 1960: "I do think that parties are important in that they tell something about the program and something about the man. Abraham Lincoln was a great president of all the people; but he was selected by his party at a key time in history because his party stood for something. The Democratic Party in this century has stood for something. It has stood for progress; it has stood for concern for the people's welfare. It has stood for a strong foreign policy and a strong national defense...."

"The role of the Democratic Party, the reason it has outlived the Federal Party, the Whig Party, and now holds responsibility in the executive branch and in the House and Senate, after this long history, has been because it has believed in moving out, in moving ahead, in starting on new areas, and bringing new programs here and abroad."

A reporter once asked Kennedy, "The Republican National Committee recently adopted a resolution saying you were pretty much of a failure. How do you feel about that?" to which he replied, "I assume it passed unanimously."

Kennedy spoke on liberalism as he accepted the New York Liberal Party nomination on September 14, 1960:

"What do our opponents mean when they apply to us the label 'Liberal'? If by 'Liberal' they mean, as they want people to believe, someone who is soft in his policies abroad, who is against local government, and who is unconcerned with the taxpayer's dollar, then the record of this party and its members demonstrate that we are not that kind of 'Liberal.' But if by a 'Liberal' they mean someone who looks ahead and not behind, someone who welcomes new ideas without rigid reactions, someone who cares about the welfare of the people–their health, their housing, their schools, their jobs, their civil rights, and their civil liberties–someone who believes we can break through the stalemate and suspicions that grip us in our policies abroad, if that is what they mean by a 'Liberal,' then I'm proud to say I'm a 'Liberal.' "

"This is my political credo: I believe in human dignity as the source of national purpose, in human liberty as the source of national action, in the human heart as the source of national compassion, and in the human mind as the source of our invention and our ideas. It is, I believe, the faith in our fellow citizens as individuals and as people that lies at the heart of the liberal faith. For liberalism is not so much a party creed or set of fixed platform promises as it is an attitude of mind and heart, a faith in man's ability through the experiences of his reason and judgment to increase for himself and his fellow men the amount of justice and freedom and brotherhood which all human life deserves."

Kennedy's reply to female delegates to the United Nations on the prospect of a female president:

"I'm always rather nervous about how you talk about women who are active in politics, whether they want to be talked about as women or as politicians."

"It was early in the seventeenth century that Francis Bacon remarked on three recent inventions already transforming the world: the compass, gunpowder, and the printing press. Now the links between the nations first forged by the compass have made us all citizens of the world, the hopes and threats of one becoming the hopes and threats of us all. In that one world's efforts to live together, the evolution of gunpowder to its ultimate limit has warned mankind of the terrible consequences of failure. And so it is to the printing press–to the recorder of man's deeds, the keeper of his conscience, the courier of his news–that we look for strength and assistance, confident that with your help man will be what he was born to be: free and independent."

"Without debate, without criticism, no administration and no country can succeed–and no republic can survive."

"I am reading it more and enjoying it less," Kennedy once said of his presidential press coverage.

"It is true that my predecessor did not object as I do to pictures of one's golfing skill in action. But neither on the other hand did he ever bean a Secret Service man."

During a press conference in March 1962, a reporter chided the president for changing his position on a particular issue, and asked whether Kennedy planned to "eat his words." Kennedy replied, "Well, I'm going to have a dinner for all the people who've written [that I would retract my statement] and we'll see who eats what!"

Kennedy shared his idea of a good news day in a 1962 issue of *Parade* magazine: "To paraphrase the old saying, 'Good news is no news.'"

Kennedy was surprised when *The New York Times* endorsed him for president. After the election, Kennedy said, "In part, at least, I am one person who can truthfully say, 'I got my job through *The New York Times.*'"

"There is a terrific disadvantage in not having the abrasive quality of the press applied to you daily. Even though we never like it, and even though we wish they didn't write it, and even though we disapprove, there isn't any doubt that we could not do the job at all in a free society without a very, very active press."

"No president should fear public scrutiny of his program. For from that scrutiny comes understanding; and from that understanding comes support or opposition. And both are necessary."

In a 1961 address to the American Newspaper Publishers Association, Kennedy joked with the audience, most of whom had supported Nixon rather than Kennedy in the 1960 election:

"When a well-known diplomat from another country demanded recently that our State Department repudiate certain newspaper attacks on his colleague, it was necessary for us to reply that this administration was not responsible for the press, for the press had already made it clear that it was not responsible for this administration."

In the same address, Kennedy asked the publishers to exercise caution and to properly censor themselves.

"I do ask every publisher, every editor, and every newsman in the nation to reexamine his own standards, and to recognize the nature of our country's peril. In time of war, the government and the press have customarily joined in an effort based largely on self-discipline, to prevent unauthorized disclosures to the enemy. In time of 'clear and present danger,' the courts have held that even the privileged rights of the First Amendment must yield to the public's need for national security."

"I am asking the members of the newspaper profession and the industry in this country to reexamine their own responsibilities, to consider the degree and the nature of the present danger, and to heed the duty of self-restraint which that danger imposes upon us all."

"I am not asking your newspapers to support the administration, but I am asking your help in the tremendous task of informing and alerting the American people. For I have complete confidence in the response and dedication of our citizens whenever they are fully informed."

"For the facts of the matter are that this nation's foes have openly boasted of acquiring through our newspapers information they would otherwise hire agents to acquire through theft, bribery, or espionage; that details of this nation's covert preparations to counter the enemy's covert operations have been available to every newspaper reader, friend and foe alike; that the size, the strength, the location, and the nature of our forces and weapons, and our plans and strategy for their use, have all been pinpointed in the press and other news media to a degree sufficient to satisfy any foreign power; and that, in at least in one case, the publication of details concerning a secret mechanism whereby satellites were followed required its alteration at the expense of considerable time and money. The newspapers which printed these stories were loyal, patriotic, responsible, and well-meaning. Had we been engaged in open warfare, they undoubtedly would not have published such items. But in the absence of open warfare, they recognized only the tests of journalism and not the tests of national security. And my question tonight is whether additional tests should not now be adopted.

"The question is for you alone to answer. No public official should answer it for you. No governmental plan should impose its restraints against your will. But I would be failing in my duty to the nation, in considering all of the responsibilities that we now bear and all of the means at hand to meet those responsibilities, if I did not commend this problem to your attention, and urge its thoughtful consideration."

Kennedy on America

K ennedy spoke in Washington the day before announcing his candidacy for the presidency:

"The American purpose remains what it has been since the nation's founding: to demonstrate that the organization of men and societies on the basis of human freedom is not an absurdity, but an enriching, ennobling, practical achievement. So long as there are slums in which people have to live, so long as there are schools that are overcrowded or antiquated or inadequate, so long as there are men in search of decent jobs and homes, so long as there are sick people in need of medical care, so long as anyone suffers discrimination by reason of color, race, religion, or national origin, the work of America is not done."

Speaking at commencement at American University in Washington in June 1963:

"Our problems are man-made—therefore, they can be solved by man. And man can be as big as he wants. No problem of human destiny is beyond human beings. Man's reason and spirit have often solved the seemingly unsolvable—and we believe they can do it again."

"We are not afraid to entrust the American people with unpleasant facts, foreign ideas, alien philosophies, and competitive values. For a nation that is afraid to let its people judge the truth and falsehood in an open market is a nation that is afraid of its people."

"If we are to give the leadership the world requires of us, we must be true to the great principles of our Constitution—the very principles which distinguish us from our adversaries in the world."

From a speech to Congress in 1961:

"We stand, as we have always stood from our earliest beginnings, for the independence and equality of all nations. This nation was born of revolution and raised in freedom. And we do not intend to leave an open road for despotism."

From a speech at Independence Hall in Philadelphia on July 4, 1962:
"The greatest works of our nation's founders lay not in documents and in declarations, but in creative, determined action."

"Let us once again transform the American continent into a vast crucible of revolutionary ideas and efforts–a tribute to the power of the creative energies of free men and women–an example to all the world that liberty and progress walk hand in hand. Let us once again awaken our American revolution until it guides the struggle of people everywhere–not with an imperialism of force or fear–but the rule of courage and freedom and hope for the future of man."

"The United States did not rise to greatness by waiting for others to lead."

"Every great age is marked by innovation and daring—by the ability to meet unprecedented problems with intelligent solutions. In a time of turbulence and change, it is more true than ever that knowledge is power; for only by true understanding and steadfast judgment are we able to master the challenge of history.   If this is so, we must strive to acquire knowledge—and to apply it with wisdom. We must reject over-simplified theories of international life—the theory that American power is unlimited, or that the American mission is to remake the world in the American image. We must seize the vision of a free and diverse world—and shape our policies to speed progress toward a more flexible world order."

"What we need now in this nation, more than atomic power, or air power, or financial, industrial, or even manpower, is brain power. What we need most of all is a constant flow of new ideas—a government and a nation and a press and a public opinion which respect new ideas and respect the people who have them."

"The United States has to move very fast to even stand still."

In an address to the United Nations General Assembly on September 20, 1963, Kennedy spoke on the power of the American people: "Never before has man had such capacity to control his own destiny, to end thirst and hunger, to conquer poverty and disease, to banish illiteracy and massive human misery. We have the power to make this the best generation of mankind in the history of the world—or make it the last."

"It is the fate of this generation . . . to live with a struggle we did not start, in a world we did not make."

"Things do not happen. Things are made to happen."

"If we are faithful to our past, we cannot be fearful of our future."

"History is a relentless master. It has no present, only the past rushing into the future.

To try to hold fast is to be swept aside."

"We would like to live as we once lived, but history will not permit it."

"I really don't look to the past. I look to the present."

"Our nation is commissioned by history to be either an observer of freedom's failure or the cause of its success."

"Our national strength matters, but the spirit which informs and controls our strength matters just as much."

"The American, by nature, is optimistic. He is experimental, an inventor and a builder who builds best when called upon to build greatly. Arouse his will to believe in himself, give him a great goal to believe in, and he will create the means to reach it."

"We love our country, not for what it was, though it has always been great—not for what it is, though of this we are deeply proud—but for what it someday can and, through the efforts of us all, someday will be."

"We must look to long days ahead, which if we are courageous and persevering can bring us what we all desire."

"Let our patriotism be reflected in the creation of confidence rather than crusades of suspicion. Let us prove we think our country great by striving to make it greater. And, above all, let us remember that, however serious the outlook, the one great irreversible trend in world history is on the side of liberty—and so, for all time to come, are we."

"A man may die, nations may rise and fall, but an idea lives on."

"It is not our military might or our higher standard of living that has most distinguished us from our adversaries. It is our belief that the state is the servant of the citizen and not its master."

"Let us resolve to be masters, not the victims, of our history, controlling our own destiny without giving way to blind suspicions and emotions."

"I am certain that after the dust of centuries has passed over our cities, we too will be remembered not for victories or defeats in battle or in politics, but for our contribution to the human spirit."

From an address in Frankfurt, Germany, in 1963 entitled "A New Social Order": "For time and the world do not stand still. Change is the law of life. And those who look only to the past or the present are certain to miss the future."

"The men who create power make an indispensable contribution to the nation's greatness, but the men who question power make a contribution just as indispensable, especially when that questioning is disinterested, for they determine whether we use power or power uses us."

"We must face the fact that the United States is neither omnipotent nor omniscient—that we are only six percent of the world's population . . . and that therefore there cannot be an American solution to every world problem."

"We don't see the end of the tunnel, but I must say I don't think it is darker than it was a year ago, and in some ways lighter."

"Every time that we try to lift a problem from our own shoulders, and shift that problem to the hands of the government, to the same extent we are sacrificing the liberties of our people."

"The quality of American life must keep pace with the quantity of American goods. This country cannot afford to be materially rich and spiritually poor."

"Wisdom requires the long view. And the long view shows us that the revolution of national independence is a fundamental fact of our era. This revolution will not be stopped. As new nations emerge from the oblivion of centuries, their first aspiration is to affirm their national identity. Their deepest hope is for a world where, within a framework of international cooperation, every country can solve its own problems according to its own traditions and ideals."

"I sometimes think that we are impressed too much by the clamor of daily urgencies. The newspaper headlines and the television screen give us the short view. They so flood us with stop-press detail that we lose sight of the grand movements of history. Yet it is the profound tendencies, and not the passing excitements, that will shape the future."

"The United States... does have a special responsibility in the world. It is, in fact, a threefold responsibility: a responsibility to our citizens, a responsibility to the people of the whole world who are affected by our decisions, and to the next generation of humanity."

"No nation, large or small, can be indifferent to the fate of others, near or far."

"So let us not be petty when our cause is so great. Let us not quarrel amongst ourselves when our nation's future is at stake. Let us stand together with renewed confidence in our cause—united in our heritage of the past and our hopes for the future—and determined that this land we love shall lead all mankind into new frontiers of peace and abundance."

"The problems of the world cannot possibly be solved by skeptics or cynics, whose horizons are limited by the obvious realities. We need men who can dream of things that never were."

"We sometimes chafe at the burden of our obligations, the complexity of our decisions, the agony of our choices. But there is no comfort or security for us in evasion, no solution in abdication, no relief in irresponsibility."

"We are not fifty countries—we are one country of fifty states and one people. And I believe that those programs which make life better for some of our people will make life better for all of our people."

The Uncommon Wisdom of John F. Kennedy

"A nation reveals itself not only by the men it produces but also by the men it honors, the men it remembers."

The Kennedy Wit

Laughter was important to Kennedy. He once gave a silver beer mug to a good friend, with the inscription:

There are three things which are real:
God, human folly, and laughter.
The first two are beyond our comprehension
So we must do what we can with the third.

Upon receiving an honorary degree from Yale University in 1962, Kennedy joked, "It might be said now that I have the best of both worlds. A Harvard education and a Yale degree."

On the campaign trail, in Maryland, Kennedy spoke about Nikita Khrushchev:

"I know something about Mr. Khrushchev, whom I met a year ago in the Senate Foreign

Relations Committee, and I know something about the nature and history of his country, which I visited in 1939. Mr. Khrushchev himself, it is said, told the story a few years ago about the Russian who began to run through the Kremlin, shouting, 'Khrushchev is a fool! Khrushchev is a fool!' He was sentenced, the premier said, to twenty-three years in prison, 'three for insulting the party secretary, and twenty for revealing a state secret.'"

Kennedy met with Khrushchev in Vienna in June 1961. In the midst of discussing a ban on nuclear testing, Kennedy quoted an old Chinese proverb: "'The journey of a thousand miles begins with one step.'"

Khrushchev was impressed. "You seem to know the Chinese very well," he said.

"We may both get to know them better," replied Kennedy.

On the night of his inauguration, Kennedy told a reporter, "The Johnsons and I have been to five balls tonight, and we still have one unfulfilled ambition—and that is to see somebody dance."

Kennedy on baseball: "Last year, more Americans went to symphonies than went to baseball games. This may be viewed as an alarming statistic, but I think that both baseball and the country will endure."

"I am sorry to say that there is too much point to the wisecrack that life is extinct on other planets because their scientists were more advanced than ours."

Kennedy joked about one of his White House predecessors, President Harry S. Truman, at his 1962 inaugural anniversary dinner.

"I must say it is nice to have a former president who speaks well of you, and we are glad to have him here tonight. His only request has been, since I have been president, to get his piano up from the cellar, and we have done that–and we are going to run on it."

"I have sent [former president Truman] the following wire: 'Dear Mr. President: I have noted with interest your suggestion as to where those who vote for my opponent should go. While I understand and sympathize with your deep motivation, I think it is important that our side try to refrain from raising the religious issue."

"It has recently been observed that whether I serve one or two terms in the presidency, I will find myself at the end of that period at what might be called an awkward age—too old to begin a new career, and too young to write my memoirs."

Addressing the graduating class at West Point, Kennedy wished the cadets qualified success:

"I'm not unmindful of the fact that two graduates of the Academy [Ulysses S. Grant and Dwight D. Eisenhower] have reached the White House, and neither was a member of my party. Until I'm more certain that this trend will be broken, I wish that all of you may be generals and not commanders in chief."

Kennedy liked to kid around with the White House correspondents. On the issue of school prayer and its exclusion from an education bill then before Congress: "Speaking of the religious issue, I asked the chief justice tonight whether he thought our new education bill was constitutional, and he said: 'It's clearly constitutional—it hasn't got a prayer.' "

Early in his presidency, a reporter asked Kennedy, "If you had to do it over again, would you work for the presidency and would you recommend the job to others?"

Kennedy replied, "Well, the answer to the first question is yes, and the answer to the second is no. I don't recommend it to others, at least not for a while."

In February 1961, Kennedy told the National Industrial Conference Board in Washington:

"It would be premature to ask for your support in the next election, and it would be inaccurate to thank you for it in the past."

Kennedy took Indian Prime Minister Nehru on a boat ride past the luxurious mansions of Newport, Rhode Island. As they passed mansion after mansion, Kennedy said to Nehru:

"I wanted you to see how the average American family lives."

At a press conference held in Anchorage, Alaska, in 1960:

QUESTION: Senator, you were promised a military intelligence briefing from the president. Have you received that?

KENNEDY: Yes. I talked on Thursday morning to General Wheeler from the Defense Department.

QUESTION: What was his first name?

KENNEDY: He didn't brief me on that.

Especially at his earliest press conferences, Kennedy read his prepared answers from index cards. One reporter noted that when he was a senator, Kennedy had been far more informal with the press. Why had he decided to use nothing but prepared answers?

"Because," Kennedy replied, "I'm not a textual deviant."

Senator Kennedy, on his roots: "I come from that section of the country where many school-children have never seen a cow and the only things that farmers raise are their hats."

Kennedy observed during his 1962 address at

the University of California at Berkeley, "This has been a week of momentous events around the world. The long and painful struggle in Algeria which comes to an end. Both nuclear powers and neutrals labored at Geneva for a solution to the problem of a spiraling arms race, and also to the problems which so vex our relations with the Soviet Union. The Congress opened hearings on a trade bill which is far more than a trade bill, but an opportunity to build a stronger and closer Atlantic Community. And my wife had her first and last ride on an elephant!"

At an inaugural ceremony for new electric generators at the Green River in the Colorado River Basin in September 1963, Kennedy was about to pull a switch that would activate the generators 150 miles away:

"I never know when I press these whether I am going to blow up Massachusetts or start the project."

At City Hall in Cork, Ireland, in 1963, Kennedy quipped:

"I don't want to give the impression that every

member of this administration in Washington is Irish. It just seems that way."

Asked if he had heard of the huge-selling recording, *The First Family*, on which Vaughan Meader performed spot-on impressions of Kennedy, the president replied, "Yes, I have... listened to Mr. Meader's record, but I thought it sounded more like Teddy than me, so he's annoyed."

Kennedy said of Paris in 1961:

"This city is no stranger to me. A Parisian designed the city of Washington. He laid out our broad boulevards after living in this community. When he had finished his generous design, he presented a bill to the Congress for $90,000, and the Congress of the United States, in one of those bursts of economic fervor for which they are justifiably famous, awarded him the munificent sum of $3,000. Some people have been so unkind as to suggest that your clothes designers have been collecting his bill ever since."

At the inaugural anniversary dinner on January 20, 1962, attended by such luminaries as Danny Thomas, President Harry S. Truman, and Rosemary Clooney, Kennedy in part gave a dry parody of his famous inaugural address of the previous year:

"I spoke a year ago today, to take the Inaugural, and I would like to paraphrase a couple of statements I made that day by saying that we observe tonight not a celebration of freedom but a victory of party, for we have sworn to pay off the same party debt our forebears ran up nearly a year and three months ago.

"Our deficit will not be paid off in the next hundred days, nor will it be paid off in the first one thousand days, nor in the life of this administration. Nor perhaps even in our lifetime on this planet, but let us begin—remembering that generosity is not a sign of weakness and that ambassadors are always subject to Senate confirmation, for if the Democratic Party cannot be helped by the many who are poor, it cannot be saved by the few who are rich."

The Personal Kennedy

From a speech at the America's Cup race in Newport, Rhode Island, in 1962: "I really don't know why it is that all of us are so committed to the sea, except I think it is because in addition to the fact that the sea changes and the light changes, and ships change, it is because we all came from the sea. And it is an interesting biological fact that all of us have in our veins the exact same percentage of salt in our blood that exists in the ocean, and, therefore, we have salt in our blood, in our sweat, in our tears. We are tied to the ocean. And when we go back to the sea, whether it is to sail or to watch it, we are going back from whence we came."

192   "The courage of life is often a less dramatic spectacle than the courage of a final moment; but it is no less than a magnificent mixture of triumph and tragedy."

"What really counts is not the immediate act of courage or of valor, but those who bear the struggle day in and day out–not the sunshine patriots but those who are willing to stand for a long period of time."

"Perfect valor consists in doing without witnesses that which we would be capable of doing before everyone."

"Life is never easy. There is work to be done and obligations to be met—obligations to truth, to justice, and to liberty."

"Only those who dare to fail greatly can ever achieve greatly."

"Do not pray for easy lives. Pray to be stronger men."

"Once you say you're going to settle for second, that's what happens to you in life, I find."

"Failure has no friends."

"The great enemy of the truth is very often not the lie… but the myth."

"Nothing is more stirring than the recognition of great public purpose."

From Kennedy's final State of the Union address in 1963: "Difficult days need not be dark."

"We must use time as a tool, not as a crutch."

"To state the facts frankly is not to despair the future nor indict the past. The prudent heir takes careful inventory of his legacies and gives a faithful accounting to those whom he owes an obligation of trust."

"Forgive your enemies, but never forget their names."

"Too often we...enjoy the comfort of opinion without the discomfort of thought."

"Conformity is the enemy of thought and the jailer of freedom."

"Every apparent blessing contains the seeds of danger, every area of trouble gives out a ray of hope; and the one unchangeable certainty is that nothing is certain or unchangeable."

"When written in Chinese, the word 'crisis' is composed of two characters: One represents danger and one represents opportunity."

On Thanksgiving Day, Kennedy issued a proclamation from the White House in which he asked the people to be grateful for their many blessings: "We must never forget that the highest appreciation is not to utter words, but to live by them."

"When at some future date the high court of history sits in judgment on each of us, recording whether in our brief span of service we fulfilled our responsibilities to the state, our success or failure, in whatever office we hold, will be measured by the answers to four questions: First, were we truly men of courage?... Second, were we truly men of judgment?... Third, were we truly men of integrity?... Finally, were we truly men of dedication?"

196 On the presidency: "Sure, it's a big job; but I don't know anyone who can do it better than I can."

"My imagination makes me human and makes me a fool; it gives me all the world and exiles me from it."

"I am an idealist without illusions."

"You've got to live every day like it's your last day on earth."

November 22, 1963

P resident Kennedy had planned to deliver a pair of speeches on the day of his assassination. Highlights of these never-delivered speeches:

"In a world of complex and continuing problems, in a world full of frustrations and irritations, America's leadership must be guided by the lights of learning and reason or else those who confuse rhetoric with reality and the plausible with the possible will gain the popular ascendancy with their seemingly swift and simple solutions to every world problem."

"For this nation's strength and security are not easily or cheaply obtained, nor are they quickly and simply explained. There are many kinds of strength and no one kind will suffice."

The Uncommon Wisdom of John F. Kennedy

"If we are strong, our strength will speak for itself. If we are weak, words will be of no help."

Recognizing America's progress in space:
"There is no longer any doubt about the strength and skill of American science, American industry, American education, and the American free enterprise system. In short, our national space effort represents a great gain in, and a great resource of, our national strength...."

"Only an America which practices what it preaches about equal rights and social justice will be respected by those whose choice affects our future. Only an America which has fully educated its citizens is fully capable of tackling the complex problems and perceiving the hidden dangers of the world in which we live. And only an America which is growing and prospering economically can sustain the worldwide defenses of freedom, while demonstrating to all concerned the opportunities of our system and society."

November 22, 1963

"America today is stronger than ever before. Our adversaries have not abandoned their ambitions, our dangers have not diminished, our vigilance cannot be relaxed. But now we have the military, the scientific, and the economic strength to do whatever must be done for the preservation and promotion of freedom. That strength will never be used in pursuit of aggressive ambitions–it will always be used in pursuit of peace. It will never be used to promote provocations–it will always be used to promote the peaceful settlement of disputes."

"We in this country, in this generation, are–by destiny rather than choice–the watchmen on the walls of world freedom."

"Freedom is the way to the future, an America which is known to be first in the effort for peace as well as preparedness."

"There is no noncontroversial way to fulfill our constitutional pledge to establish justice and promote domestic tranquillity, but we intend to fulfill those obligations because they are right."

"For this country is moving and it must not stop. It cannot stop. For this is a time for courage and a time for challenge. Neither conformity nor complacency will do. Neither the fanatics nor the fainthearted are needed. And our duty as a party is not to our party alone, but to the nation, and, indeed, to all mankind. Our duty is not merely the preservation of political power but the preservation of peace and freedom. So let us not be petty when our cause is so great. Let us not quarrel amongst ourselves when our nation's future is at stake. Let us stand together with renewed confidence in our cause—united in our heritage of the past and our hopes for the future—and determined that this land we love shall lead all mankind into new frontiers of peace and abundance."

November 22, 1963

Epilogue

President John Fitzgerald Kennedy was laid to rest in Arlington National Cemetery on November 25, 1963. The youngest man elected president of the United States of America was tragically the youngest man to die in office. The inscription at Kennedy's grave site, taken from his 1961 inaugural address, reads:

Let the word go forth
From this time and place
To friend and foe alike
That the torch has been passed
To a new generation of Americans.

Let every nation know
Whether it wishes us well or ill
That we shall pay any price—bear any burden

Meet any hardship–support any friend
Oppose any foe to assure the survival
And the success of liberty

Now the trumpet summons us again
Not as a call to bear arms
–though embattled we are
But a call to bear the burden of a long twilight
struggle
A struggle against the common enemies of man
Tyranny–Poverty–Disease–and War itself

In the long history of the world
Only a few generations have been granted
The role of defending freedom
In the hour of maximum danger
I do not shrink from this responsibility
I welcome it

The Energy–the Faith–the Devotion
Which we bring to this endeavor
Will light our country
And all who serve it
And the glow from that fire
Can truly light the world

Epilogue

And so my fellow Americans
Ask not what your country can do for you
Ask what you can do for your country
My fellow citizens of the world–ask not
What America can do for you–but what together
We can do for the freedom of man

With a good conscience our only sure reward
With history the final judge of our deeds
Let us go forth to lead the land we love–asking
His blessing
And His help–but knowing that here on earth
God's work must truly be our own.

The Life of
John Fitzgerald Kennedy
———— *1917–1963* ————

May 29, 1917

John Fitzgerald Kennedy is born in Brookline, Massachusetts, to Joseph P. Kennedy and Rose Fitzgerald Kennedy.

1935

Studies at the London School of Economics during the summer.

Enters Princeton University, but leaves after an attack of jaundice during his freshman year.

1936

Enters Harvard University.

1937

Visits Europe with his father, at the time the United States ambassador to England.

June 1940

Graduates cum laude from Harvard University.

July 1940

Kennedy's college thesis published as a book titled *Why England Slept.*

September 1941

Sworn in as an ensign in the United States Navy.

March 1943

Given command of *PT-109* as a lieutenant.

August 1943

PT-109 sunk by a Japanese destroyer; Kennedy performs heroically in saving his fellow crew members.

June 11, 1944

Receives Purple Heart for his actions after the sinking of *PT-109*.

November 5, 1946

Wins election to the House of Representatives as a congressman from the Eleventh District of Massachusetts. Wins reelection in 1948 and 1950.

November 4, 1952

Wins election to the U.S. Senate. Is reelected in 1958.

September 12, 1953

Marries Jacqueline Lee Bouvier.

1956

Profiles in Courage, written by Kennedy while recovering from back surgery, is published. It wins the Pulitzer Prize for biography in 1957.

August 17, 1956

Loses bid to become the Democratic nominee for vice president.

August 23, 1956

Jacqueline Kennedy gives birth to the Kennedys' first child, a daughter, who dies on the same day.

November 27, 1957

Caroline Bouvier Kennedy born.

January 2, 1960

Announces candidacy for president of the United States.

July 13, 1960
Receives Democratic nomination for president.

November 8, 1960
Defeats Richard Nixon to become the thirty-
fifth president of the United States.

November 25, 1960
John Fitzgerald Kennedy Jr. born.

January 20, 1961
Inauguration Day.

March 1, 1961
Signs bill creating the Peace Corps.

April 17, 1961
The Bay of Pigs invasion of Cuba.

May 25, 1961

Delivers speech committing the nation "to achieving the goal, before this decade is out, of landing a man on the moon and returning him safely to the earth."

June 3–4, 1961

Meets with Nikita Khrushchev in Vienna.

July 25, 1961

Delivers address on the Berlin Crisis, declaring, "Our presence in West Berlin, and our access thereto, cannot be ended by any act of the Soviet government."

October 16–28, 1962

Cuban Missile Crisis.

June 26, 1963

Delivers *"Ich bin ein Berliner"* speech in West Germany.

August 5, 1963

Signs Limited Test Ban Treaty in Moscow.

August 7, 1963

Patrick Bouvier Kennedy born. He dies just two days later.

November 22, 1963

Kennedy fatally shot in downtown Dallas.

ALL PHOTOGRAPHS APPEAR COURTESY OF
THE JOHN FITZGERALD KENNEDY LIBRARY, BOSTON.

FABIAN BACHRACH, WHITE HOUSE

44

ROBERT KNUDSEN, WHITE HOUSE

52, 94, 152

ABBIE ROWE, NATIONAL PARK SERVICE

84, 152

CECIL STOUGHTON, WHITE HOUSE

i, 96, 136, 166, 190, 198, 204

U. S. ARMY SIGNAL CORPS

38